The Canadian
Student Financial Survival
Guide

Also by Graham McWaters

The Canadian Retirement Guide

The Retirement Guide

The Canadian
Student
Financial Survival
Guide

A comprehensive handbook on
financing your education, managing
your expenses & planning for
a debt-free future

Graham McWaters and
Winthrop Sheldon

INSOMNIAC PRESS

Library and Archives Canada Cataloguing in Publication

McWaters, Graham, 1956-
    The Canadian student financial survival guide : a comprehensive handbook on financing your education, managing your expenses & planning for a debt-free future / Graham McWaters and Winthrop Sheldon.

Includes bibliographical references and index.
ISBN 1-897178-03-4

    1. College students--Canada--Finance, Personal. 2. College costs-Canada. I. Sheldon, Winthrop, 1982- II. Title.

HG179.M367 2005   332.024'0088'378198   C2005-904235-4
The publisher gratefully acknowledges the support of the Canada Council, the Ontario Arts Council and the Department of Canadian Heritage through the Book Publishing Industry Development Program.

Printed and bound in Canada

Insomniac Press
192 Spadina Avenue, Suite 403
Toronto, Ontario, Canada, M5T 2C2
www.insomniacpress.com

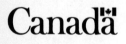

Dedicated to:

My parents, Abby and Maxwell, for their advice and counsel throughout my four-year university experience, and for inspiring me to take chances. (Win Sheldon)

My patient and understanding wife, Angie, and my two very active sons, Matthew and Ryan, for their constant support and unconditional love. (Graham McWaters)

Disclaimer

While every effort was made to ensure the accuracy of the information herein, the authors and the publisher assume no responsibility for errors, omissions, inconsistencies, or changes, and they disclaim any liability arising from the use of information in this book. Every person's situation is different and it is always prudent to consult qualified professionals and relevant organizations.

Acknowledgments

The research for this project was compiled by twenty Bachelor of Commerce students from McGill University and one financial planner. In addition, the guide was edited and prepared by parents that have assisted their children on the path to a university education as well as those just starting the savings mode. Eighteen of the BComm students were actively pursuing their studies while they completed their research. The students came from different backgrounds and they all landed at McGill through different means of financial arrangements such as student loans, RESPs, savings, family assistance, scholarships, grants, and other forms of credit. The students were living in many forms of accommodation such as on-campus residence, single apartments, shared accommodation, and some were living at home. Based upon their real-life experiences and their thorough research, they were able to assist in putting together *The Canadian Student Financial Survival Guide*.

Winthrop Sheldon (BComm '05) and Graham McWaters (BComm '80) were able to assemble this group through the assistance of the business fraternity, Alpha Kappa Psi, Phi Chi chapter. Special mention also goes out to Murray Morton for his contribution to the chapter on financial planning and to Paul Vincent (BComm '81) for his contribution to the chapter on credit. The guide was also reviewed by Andrew Gianou, Peter Gianou, Tammi Turgeon, and Chris Yates. Andrew is a current BComm student at McGill. Peter recently put two of his children through two completely different post-secondary educational programs and has a thorough knowledge of the various expenses associated with this costly venture. Tammi has had two post-secondary experiences: one in 1990 and she recently received her Bachelor of Education. She is currently planning and preparing to assist her two children through their post-secondary education. Chris is just starting his post-secondary experience.

The group of McGill students includes: Gabriel Araish, Christopher Baker, Hugo Bergeron Marier, Danielle Carrie, Linda Dang, Sean Gallagher, Sylvain Gervais, Linda Grey-Noble, Dan Kenzhebayev, Gregory Leshchuk, Cathy McRoy, Matt Mendell,

Jennifer Sheng, Rogerald Solmerano, Pierre Tarantelli, Peter Thibodeau, and Jason Weinstein. Danielle Carrie is studying towards a Bachelor of Arts degree. The guide could not have been done without the contributions of these dedicated students and the great organizational skills of Winthrop Sheldon.

We hope you enjoy this comprehensive handbook on financing your education, managing your expenses, and planning for a debt-free future.

Table of Contents

Introduction

Making the decision to continue your education after graduating from high school is a great accomplishment in itself. As you plan and prepare to attend a post-secondary school, such as a college or university, or if you are already attending a post-secondary institution, you are faced with the need to finance all aspects of your education. From tuition to transportation to your books and food, there is always money being spent on something every day.

Working towards a post-secondary education is one of the most important things you can do to enhance your opportunity for a better career, but it isn't as easy as many people think, especially when it comes to the finance side of things. Young adults today are faced with ever-rising costs of tuition and the decisions made as to how to pay for school are important. The costs of college or university are prohibitive to some and very intimidating to others. It is critical for young people today to have a handle on their finances and to have a reasonable plan in order to eliminate these fears and embark on a life of financial freedom.

With tuition fees, books, accommodation, transportation, food, clothing, entertainment, and other miscellaneous expenses continually increasing, it is extremely important that you plan your finances and budget appropriately. Without a comprehensive plan in place, young people risk making short-term decisions with disastrous consequences on their long-term financial health. It can take years to fix a damaged credit rating. *The Canadian Student Financial Survival Guide* covers topics such as planning and budgeting, how to pay for your education, student loans, credit-card issues, car expenses, accommodation, and many other financial-related issues for the young person dealing with their first major finance decisions. In addition, the guide will show you how to get your first full-time job. The guide ends with an in-depth overview of financial planning.

Starting out on the right foot will assist the new graduate so they are prepared to enter the workforce. The information in this well-researched guide will not only assist you immediately but will also help you to set a solid finance foundation for your future planning, spending, and budgeting. Whether you are entering a post-secondary institution or graduate school in the near future or asserting your independence as a young adult, *The Canadian Student Financial Survival Guide* is a critical reference guide if you want to have peace of mind going forward into your financial future.

Chapter One
Planning and Budgeting

Emerging from high school, the world can be a daunting place. With many options to choose from, one can quickly become confused and unsure about how to approach the future. Proper planning will allow you to make better decisions and move easily into the future. Planning allows you to be better prepared and confident in life. To find success you must always stay ahead of the game by anticipating choices and understanding how decisions today affect your direction in life.

The first decision a young person is faced with upon graduation from high school concerns the choice between finding a job or continuing one's education, usually by attending a college or university. However, these decisions are not a means to an end on their own. Tied in to each are a multitude of factors that one needs to plan for properly:

- How will I pay for school?
- How will I afford living on my own?
- Should I live in residence?
- What type of employment will I seek when I graduate?

These are only a few of the many factors one needs to be aware of and to plan for properly in order to make informed choices to begin an enjoyable life.

Why Plan?

Everyone should consider planning as a necessity. Studies show that people who plan are more likely to get ahead and accomplish the goals they set. Planning goes further than just this; people who plan properly lead less-stressed lives and feel confident about the choices they make as they journey through life. For example, while at university, the intended goal is to graduate and get a job. However, during these years it is also possible to live a fun life, enjoying entertainment and socialization with fellow students. Whether it is out on the town, at the movies, or in an apartment with a home entertainment system, adequate planning can enable a person to lead the life they desire.

...and If You Don't Plan?

A lack of planning has many negative consequences that can be easily avoided. Having few or no plans often induces stress because without planning, a person ventures blindly into the world. However, the consequences can be even more severe than just psychological stress. Not having a plan often implies a person is not aware of all the options available to them, causing one to easily miss out on opportunities or to inadvertently "close doors in their future."

For example, most students who choose to attend university experience both living away from home and having their own credit card for the first time. With this newfound independence, many get trapped by accumulating large credit-card debt. Many students do not perceive this as a trap, for the credit-card company may not comment on one's debt, allowing it to continue to accumulate. The average student escalates this problem by planning to deal with it after graduation, when they have a "real" job to pay off the debt. This debt, however, will place limits on the individual before they are able to pay it off. For example, once this "real" job has been obtained, one may need a vehicle for transportation to and from work. But a large debt looming over one's head will be found during a credit check by a car dealership and this may result in the individual being denied their auto purchase.

It's Your Life!

Planning can be a difficult procedure, as you may discover below. However, before we discuss what is involved, it must be emphasized that *you* will be planning your life. This means that your opinions, wants, needs, and desires need to be a part of your plan. This also means that you must be prepared to deal with pressures that may lead you down different paths than those you anticipate. This pressure, in most cases, stems from family and it can get overwhelming, but you must remember: this is *your* life! Your life can only truly be labelled successful and enjoyable by you—the one living it. This may mean taking risks that involve learning about the type of person you are and having to turn around along the way, but this is okay. As long as you plan properly, turning around does not mean you are a failure, it simply implies having to go back to a fork in the road and choose the alternate route. Whether this is discovering you lack an interest in the subjects you initially study in school and decide to make a change or learning you prefer solitude and in turn move away from your roommates to live on your own, these decisions are merely instances in which one learns about who they are and are critical to developing into a successful adult. There are steps you can take now to help your decisions occur fluidly and successfully, allowing you a sense of confidence; these require understanding the type of person you are.

Who Am I?

Understanding your personality is a key to recognizing the aspects of life you are most interested in experiencing. Furthermore, understanding your personality will give you great insight into the type of lifestyle you want to have after graduation from university or college. It is important to acknowledge your personal traits so that you make choices that allow you and those around you to be happy. For example, if you know you are a messy, disorganized person, it is in your best interest to acknowledge this about yourself and to consider how this may affect those around you. In this way, being upfront with your soon-to-be roommates about these aspects of yourself will help you to plan and work together to avoid possible conflicts.

Personality Checklist

From the list below, check the characteristics that apply to you as an individual. The purpose of this exercise is for you to begin to think of how you are unique and what allows you to live your life enjoyably. There are no correct answers, and if you think of characteristics not listed below, write them in the blank spaces to further describe yourself.

Personality Checklist

- ☐ I enjoy getting a head start on projects
- ☐ I become overwhelmed easily
- ☐ I shut down when I get overwhelmed
- ☐ I tend to do everything last minute
- ☐ I enjoy cleaning
- ☐ I am messy
- ☐ I am responsible with money
- ☐ I spend money easily
- ☐ I enjoy large groups of people
- ☐ I often give into peer pressure
- ☐ I enjoy staying up late
- ☐ I like to get to bed early
- ☐ I like to sleep in
- ☐ I like to wake up early
- ☐ I like cooking for myself
- ☐ I don't like dealing with other people's problems
- ☐ I am loud
- ☐ I am quiet
- ☐ I like to shop
- ☐ I enjoy solidarity
- ☐ I often "go with the flow"
- ☐ I like to exercise
- ☐ I like exotic foods
- ☐ I am independent
- ☐ I am bossy
- ☐ I am assertive
- ☐ I am shy

Your Hobbies and Interests

Hobbies and interests say a lot about your individual nature and are important elements to think about when considering your future. One should try to incorporate as many of these as possible into a plan for achieving life goals, whether it be studying something that interests you or participating in a favourite hobby during your spare time. It may seem like common sense, but we often get overwhelmed with life and forget about simple things that bring us joy and are able to bring us back down to earth. For example, if you are moving away from home for the first time, you want this transition to be as smooth as possible. One aspect that often gets overlooked concerns food. Think about the types of food you like to eat. Do you enjoy exotic foods, trying different dishes whenever possible? Or do you like cooking for yourself? Your answer to these questions will have an influence on where you choose to live, whether it is near ethnic restaurants or a grocery store. Furthermore, by living in these locations you will be able to partake in activities you enjoy easily and naturally.

Hobbies and Interests Checklist

Try to list at least five of your hobbies and five of your interests. These should be activities that you have previous experience with and those you wish to undertake at some point in the future. Here are a few broad categories from which you may be able to narrow down and identify several of your own hobbies and interests: technology, environmental concerns, animals, children, arts, music, literature, athletics, travel, reading, cooking, etc.

Recognizing your own chosen hobbies and interests will give you a way to structure your life that allows you to include these into your future plans. Many people find themselves in positions where they are unable to live the life they desire because they do not plan how they will include these facets of life when they make choices concerning their future.

Hobbies

1. _____

2. _____

Interests

1. _____

2. _____

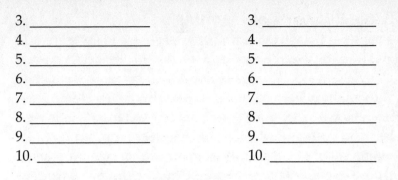

3. _____   3. _____
4. _____   4. _____
5. _____   5. _____
6. _____   6. _____
7. _____   7. _____
8. _____   8. _____
9. _____   9. _____
10. _____   10. _____

What Do You Dislike?

While understanding your interests and hobbies are important factors you should consider when planning, a conscious awareness of what you don't like can be of equal importance. For example, if you do not like messes or loud noises, then perhaps living on your own or searching for a quiet roommate similar to yourself will create the most conducive living arrangement for your lifestyle. Your dislikes should also be examined in a broader light. Becoming a doctor, for example, requires serious dedication, as it will require tremendous amounts of hard work and time. A person entering university may feel the desire and ambition to become a doctor. Whether it is because they excel at sciences or are motivated by the salary, if that person does not like physical contact with other people, they will fundamentally be unhappy working day in and day out in an occupation they don't feel comfortable with. It is these small personality quirks that must be acknowledged because they speak volumes about one's level of comfort and adaptability to their surroundings.

My Dislikes Checklist

Create a list of your dislikes. It doesn't matter what you write, these dislikes may include anything that you have an aversion to and would like to ensure is not a part of your life.

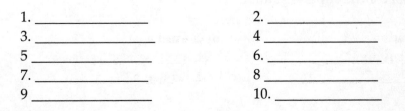

1. _____   2. _____
3. _____   4 _____
5 _____   6. _____
7. _____   8 _____
9 _____   10. _____

The Three Elements of Planning

The activity of planning during your post-secondary years will, in many ways, dictate the ease and success of the decisions you make along the way. When it is done well, students are able to study without the burden of financial concerns or demanding work schedules, and when it is done poorly, students often find their post-secondary and post-graduation years unnecessarily difficult.

Planning should be a priority no matter what stage you are at in your post-secondary preparations. Planning (for our purposes) can be divided into three parts: researching options, creating a budget, and making choices. Researching is a necessary prerequisite before any decision can be made, as one must be aware of all the available options. The next step is to create a budget. One needs to budget both their time and money so that the most realistic options may be selected from the long list created through research. After you understand the options that are realistic for you, the time comes to make your decision.

1. Researching Your Options

Brainstorm Ideas

When a person starts to research a topic, their mind is often full of wonderful ideas and many unanswered questions. Through the accumulation of research, it is easy to forget the intentions one began with. The best way to avoid this is to brainstorm as many relevant options concerning your focus and list them on a piece of paper so you may refer back to them whenever necessary. Brainstorming does not mean limiting yourself to just one topic; you can easily brainstorm broad topics, such as your future, listing your desired goals, and the different paths that will lead you there.

Below, we have listed two examples of brainstorming: one concerning education and the other concerning buying a car. Use this as an example of how you can develop relevant questions to fully investigate each option you have.

Education

Which school?

Which city?

Buying a Car

Purchase new vs. used vs. lease?

Is colour a concern?

Tuition?   Automatic vs. standard
Climate   Sedan vs. truck vs. hatchback
City life vs. rural   Air conditioning
Transportation   What type of fuel?
Courses offered (broad or not?)   Insurance, how much?
College vs. university
Athletic facilities?

Find Answers

After brainstorming, the next step of researching your options requires adequate fact finding. To research is to find all information affiliated to a given topic. There are many different methods and resources you can use to properly identify your interests: the Internet, books, magazines, television, or even by word of mouth. Another resource concerns speaking to those with experience. Whether you are trying to choose a university to attend or select a car to purchase, asking the advice of someone who has already gone through the process can provide tremendous insight. Refer back to your brainstorming sheet after completing your research so you can ensure you have found resources that cover everything you originally listed.

Stay Organized While You Research

When beginning to research, it is easy to become overwhelmed by the vast amount of resources available. The best way to keep track of all your research is to take notes, keeping track of them in an organized fashion. If you are researching by hand, then it is best to have your own notebook labelled with whatever it is you are planning for. For example, if you are planning to buy a car, you would label the book "CAR." From here on, write all things you find that pertain to buying a car into this book. If you are using a computer to store your findings, then you need to either create a file named "CAR" or a use a floppy disk reserved solely for this project. Each entry should not only be clear and precise, it should also include the resource (book title, web site, etc.), and, if applicable, the page number from which you found it. With so many resources available to exploit, it is easy to forget the source of the information you have acquired. For a resource such as a newspaper advertisement, you can even go as far as to cut the section out and keep it right in your book. So far, this might sound similar to the approach one would take in writing a term paper for school. Well, this is essentially what you are doing. When planning to write a paper, the topic must be researched first.

2. Creating a Budget

The Importance of Budgeting

Most post-secondary students today are faced with increasing financial obligations in the form of tuition hikes, soaring textbook prices, and a general increase in the cost of living as a student. Those that wish to make the most of the amazing opportunities during their post-secondary years should begin to prepare well before their applications are even sent out.

Now that you have thoroughly researched your options, it is time to figure how much they will cost. The term "cost" is used here as a term representing both money and time, two of our most limited but highly valued resources. In high school, budgeting is rarely of great concern to most students. However, upon arrival at college or university, this changes dramatically. Given a certain amount of money, it is up to the student to find a way to make the most of that money and maximize the enjoyment that they get out of it. The basics can be easily budgeted for: expenses such as groceries, rent, and utilities are often estimated for students on different university web sites and allow a rough estimate of what life at school will cost. Beyond these, funds should be budgeted for the miscellaneous expenses as mentioned previously. Lastly, students are able to decide, based on how much is left over, what types of recreational activities they are financially able to participate in. It is important to keep records of all of your expenses and to make sure that your spending is in line with the estimated budget.

As a nice starter tool, www.canlearn.ca, as well many banks, offer student budgeting templates that are very user friendly and show not only the basic components of budgeting but also the general ways in which a proper budget should be set up. The key to budgeting is not to premeditate every expense and strictly regulate what money is spent on. It is more important to avoid making the common mistake of spending without an overall plan. If all students budgeted properly, no one would have to worry about crippling credit-card debts resulting in poor credit ratings that follow them well into adult years.

Unfortunately, abusing credit has become the norm. Many students today have little or no fear of credit and abuse it in order to spend money in the short term with no regard for the long-term hazards of doing so. When using a credit card, purchases should only be made on the account when there are sufficient funds in the cardholder's bank account to immediately cover the purchase. This is one way to avoid becoming bogged down with debt. Managing credit and avoiding debt are further covered in detail in Chapter Six.

Account for All Costs

When making a budget concerning your future educational studies, we recommend you begin by making a list of all associated costs. As a high-school student living with your parents, there are many things that get done for you which are easy to forget. Sometimes we don't like to admit just how much our parents do for us until we move out and see the amount of work that it takes to live independently. Further, there are many expenses that may not be recognized while living at home. These constitute a large part of a post-secondary student's budget. These expenses can range anywhere from fees for taking part in clubs and activities to the costs of basic household goods such as light bulbs. Financial planning for post-secondary years often leaves these expenses out of the equation. Living in campus housing as a first-year student will minimize but not eliminate these types of expenses. Campus housing will often provide food as well as maintenance staff to take care of anything that needs fixing, but they do so at a premium. University residences lack personal furniture and amenities besides the basics, and cafeterias typically serve meals during short periods of the day. Money for miscellaneous food and furniture should be minimal in this setting, but there will be many other expenses depending on personal preferences and, of course, the financial situation. Intramural sports leagues, gym memberships, transportation costs, and tutorials are just some examples of things that can cost money.

For those who live off campus, realizing these costs will be all the more shocking. On top of the examples mentioned above are things such as utilities, apartment repairs, furniture of all types, tools, groceries, movie rentals, school supplies, and a whole list of other expenses that will come about. Although they are never significant on a one-by-one basis, these expenses taken as a whole can leave a student in a very rough situation if they are unprepared financially. It may be helpful to ask someone's advice at this step, as they may be able to point out some costs that you may not think of. The best resources to consult for answers to these types of questions are current students and their parents who take care of all these things, which you will soon have to take care of yourself.

Add Up All the Costs

By adding together all of the costs of your new life at college or university you will have a snapshot of how much money you need to pay for your lifestyle while there. We recommend you make a list of these costs, total them up, and compare your list to those of other students to see if you have forgotten anything (see Appendix B for a sample budget list).

Paying for the Budget

Now that all affiliated costs have been accounted for, you need to figure out whether or not you can afford them. Students and their parents should sit down and evaluate their financial picture and consider the means by which they will pay for post-secondary education. Parents should discuss with their children what portion of their child's education they are willing to pay for and make it clear when and where the line will be drawn. This should be done early enough so that the student can prepare to pay their portion of the total bill and work towards paying their share for their education if necessary. Of course, beginning to save early is always favourable from the parent's standpoint, but also from that of the student. Living at home throughout high-school years and over the summer provides the student the perfect opportunity to earn a few extra dollars to help pay for their education.

Keep in mind, every dollar saved is one less that will need to be paid back later through a student loan or other credit. Each household's saving strategy will differ depending on a number of factors, the most important of which is time. The longer the time period allotted for educational savings, the easier the process becomes. For those with the opportunity of starting their savings early, it is advantageous to consider putting away money into RESPs (Registered Education Savings Plans) or in-trust accounts. RESPs offer the benefits of tax-free growth as well as proportional contributions from the government for each year investments are made. You may also be eligible for more aid in the form of CESGs (Canadian Education Savings Grants), all of which will be discussed in later chapters.

In an ideal world, everyone would follow these guidelines; very few people actually have the luxury of being in this position. Investment strategies change for a student with no savings in their high-school years. RESPs and in-trust accounts can still be used, but it is unreasonable to believe a period of four to six years will be sufficient to pay for a university education at today's prices. It is at this point that student loans, grants, and scholarships should be considered while still attempting to save the maximum possible amount in the short term. The appropriate financial mix for different situations will be discussed in the next chapter. Be sure to compare the financial side of your plan to the time available. You may need to assess your plan from two angles:

1. How much extra time or money is required for me to pay for my plan?
2. Are there alternative routes I can take in my plan?

How Much Extra Time or Money Is Required?

After adding up the costs of college or university life and comparing them against the amount of money you will have when it is time to pay for them, it will be clear whether you need additional funds to pay for your budget. If in the end your plan is not affordable due to either monetary or time restrictions, you will then need to figure out some alternative resources that may be able to provide help. Always keep in mind the many scholarships and grant opportunities that are available to students approaching high-school graduation. Parents should inquire with their employers about scholarship opportunities. Students should research scholarships from private funds as well as provincial, federal, and university scholarship opportunities. Only after exhausting all of the outside funding possibilities and considering the significant differences in graduates' starting salaries for graduates of different post-secondary schools should certain options be completely removed from consideration. Don't forget, asking for advice can provide tremendous help. Often, when one feels stuck, it is hard to see simple solutions.

Get an Idea of How Much You Regularly Spend

You need to remember that while you have money coming into your pocket, some of it is more than likely going to be spent. You need to account for this so that you may figure out how long it will take you to save. If you do not know how much you spend on average, then you need to figure it out. If you live a fairly routine lifestyle, then it should not be difficult to reflect on your daily activities, recording the amount of money usually spent at certain places throughout the day, such as a coffee and a newspaper every morning on the way to work, a pack of cigarettes twice a week, and a tank of gas for the car every Thursday. If, however, your life does not follow a routine of some sort, then it is best to challenge yourself for a period of at least two weeks to a span of one month to record every instance you spend money, noting both what it was spent on and how much it cost. After the chosen period of time has ended, you can add up all the costs and discover what kind of spender you are and whether or not this hinders your plan. If this does hinder your plan, then you need to evaluate both the amount of money you spend and your estimated timeline.

Evaluate Your Expenses

First of all, are your expenses reasonable or are there areas in your life from which you can cut down on spending? Often it is not until someone writes down their expenses that they become aware of just how much money they spend at the snack machine in the hallway at school or how often they treat themselves to some special goody while enjoying their coffee break. If there are things that you can cut down on or eliminate, that is wonderful, you are heading toward your goal. However, if there is no cost cutting then your plan needs to be re-evaluated.

Deciding Upon an Alternative Route

If your plan doesn't seem feasible, even after considering all steps outlined above, then you need to open your book, look at your notes, and figure out any other available options. For example, is it possible to get the same degree at a different school, one closer to home or requiring fewer expenses while studying towards your degree? After making these changes to your plan, you need to once again figure out whether or not your revised plan is affordable. The purpose here is to not give up hope if the first scenario you thought about winds up being too expensive; there will be a more affordable alternative for you to choose. It will take effort to uncover such possibilities, but one of the important purposes of planning is to determine what is actually feasible; creating a budget is a key means of determining this.

Create a Timeline

When you have finally created a feasible plan, within which you account for all costs and how to pay for them, it is time to create a timeline. A timeline is an estimated projection that confirms three things: your intended goal, the plan that will get you there, and the end-date by which you expect to have your plan achieved. This timeline should be included in your initial brainstorming notes so that it is always on hand. This will enable you to confirm that you are on track and will motivate you to continue working towards your goal as you accomplish steps along the way.

3. Making Choices

After you list all of the options available to you and have accounted for the costs and ways of paying for those options, you will be well prepared to make a decision regarding your future. You will be well prepared because through brainstorming and creating a budget you critically assess how you would like to proceed before you actually do so. This is a valuable experience because you gain insight from investigating numerous possible options and then choosing those that are the most reasonable and affordable. Your ability to make a sound choice will be rooted in the accuracy of the budget you create, so we cannot stress enough the importance of approaching the budget with a serious attitude.

Furthermore, the importance of the budget you create does not stop after you have confirmed your ability to pay for your lifestyle at college or university. The budget is the feature you will continually refer to, confirming that you are on the right path. You must remember throughout this process to write everything down and to keep track of expenses, and don't forget that this should be written either in your book or your computer file—write everything down! By accounting for everything, you will know if your projections are correct and if any financial adjustments are needed.

Chapter Two
How to Pay for Your Education

For most young adults, the first major financial hurdle that must be overcome is paying for post-secondary education. As costs for college and university increase, the need to develop a full understanding of the overall cost as well as a plan to pay for this education has become an extremely important and time-consuming task. In order to gain this understanding and develop a strategy on how to pay for your education, the overall cost of all types of post-secondary education must first be discussed. You need to determine where you will attend your post-secondary studies and all the related costs in doing so. We will explore different ways to save and pay for this education. We will review scholarships, part-time jobs, ways of saving your money, RESPs, and credit. Securing a degree or certificate can set you in the direction towards a successful career and life. Anyone who desires to pursue further education should not be inhibited by financial restrictions. Everyone has options; the trick is finding the right one for you.

Cost

Before you can begin planning on how to pay for school, you first need to know how much it is going to cost you. Since the price of post-secondary education varies from student to student and from school to school, it would be impossible to present a set price that every person should save for. This section will examine the various items you need to account for in your planning and budgeting. Everything from how much you will need for school itself to the cost of basic living expenses and social outings will be discussed. It is important to get a full picture now so there are no surprises later.

When you begin to compile a list of costs, the first thing that must be taken into account is the overall cost of attending your school of choice. Of course, the bulk of this money will go towards tuition, and residence, should you decide to live on campus your first year. There is a fairly large gap between the cost of college and university. Should your financial situation be one that prohibits you from pursuing university, this may be an important fact to take into consideration. Not only does college cost less but also its programs are often shorter than those in university. It is also your responsibility to make sure that there are no hidden costs such as health insurance or student fees that are required on top of the tuition. Finally, the cost of course textbooks should be measured. To do this, find out how many courses there are in your program and allow at least $75 for each one. From our experience, new textbooks cost slightly over $100 but you can often find used textbooks for considerably less.

Another cost of post-secondary education is that of living expenses. If you are trying to keep costs at a minimum and there is no school close enough to allow you to commute to and from home, it would be recommended to choose an institution in a more rural setting. For example, the cost of student housing surrounding McGill University in Montreal is more than double than that of Bishop's University in Lennoxville, Quebec, and the situation is parallel when comparing Seneca College in Toronto to Loyalist College in Belleville, Ontario. Before deciding on any particular school, research exactly how much an apartment would cost versus your share of a house. Also account for any cost increases that may happen to your lease (generally 2% a year), as well as renters' insurance and anything not included in the lease such as utilities, phone, Internet, and cable. It is also important to consider how much food will cost each week. You could also try buying groceries while still living at home to know exactly how much they will cost you or budget around $75 to $100 a week. Eating in restaurants or buying a food plan while in residence are two other options (with the restaurants being the higher-cost choice).

You must also budget how much money you plan on spending on entertainment, eating out, renting movies, and any other out-of-pocket expenses. Keep in mind that when you begin going to college or university, it is roughly around the time that you will become of legal drinking age. This doesn't mean you have to start any bad habits. If you decide to indulge in alcoholic beverages, we recommend that you do so in moderation. If you overindulge, the cost—financially and physically—can ruin your educational plans in many ways.

Figuring out how much school will cost is not exactly a science, but if you take the time to consider all angles, your estimate can be very close to the actual cost. Be sure that when doing this to not cut any corners or sell yourself short. If you are currently consuming $90 per week in groceries, it is not safe to assume that you can live on $50 per week. Of course, part of the college/university experience is learning how to economize, but you will find that it is better to plan and prepare for a budget slightly larger than you need than it is to end up short of money. Planning ahead can help avoid any devastating surprises, not to mention it is good to get into the habit of looking ahead—your life will be going through many transitions as you begin travelling towards adulthood and working towards autonomy. (See Appendix B for a sample school budget form.)

Scholarships

Scholarships are the optimal form of financial support as they come with few to no strings attached. The money you are awarded is yours to keep; you do not have to pay it back and you especially do not have to pay any interest. In this section, we will discuss the different types of scholarships available, where to find scholarships, and we will briefly share some tips on how to position yourself and successfully apply for scholarships. Many people believe that the only people eligible for scholarships are those who show outstanding academic performance. Although it is true that academic scholarships do exist, there are also many scholarships that focus on aspects of your life that do not involve grades.

All across Canada there are scholarships available to students coming from any background. Almost all schools in Canada have entrance scholarships and major scholarships. Typically, entrance scholarships are awarded based purely on academic standing. Major scholarships, on the other hand, are awarded to students who demonstrate overall academic success plus extracurricular and community involvement. However, there are awards at most schools that come from independent organizations that give prizes to otherwise deserving students. If you are not at all academically inclined but are a very involved student or are otherwise talented, you should look at awards provided by foundations outside your school of choice. Whether you are a sports enthusiast, an "A" student, an artist, a leader, multi-talented, or simply hard-working and determined, there is a scholarship for you. The only problem is knowing where to look.

As stated before, all post-secondary institutions have awards of some kind. Once you decide where you plan on studying, your school should be the first place you look. Since there is no limit to the number of awards a particular student can apply for or win, the more you apply for the better. Your other two best resources for scholarships are your high-school guidance department for local awards and the Internet for other awards spread across the country. The Internet can be used to search for scholarships on search engines or by visiting www.scholarshipscanada.com, Canada's largest source for scholarships all in one place. On the Scholarships Canada web site, you can spend five minutes registering and a few more minutes filling out some basic information about yourself, such as academic average, interests, clubs, etc., and the search engine will come up with many potential awards. As mentioned, the more scholarships you apply for the better. Although scholarship applications may be tedious and exhausting, if done properly, the investment in time can be worthwhile and very rewarding.

While in your senior year of high school, spend some time applying for scholarships. Although you may not win them all, you may win enough to help remove some of the financial pressure of a post-secondary education. Aside from entrance scholarships that are guaranteed if you have a certain average, you are competing against other applicants for only one award. Keeping this in mind, there are three steps that can be taken to better your chances and increase the ease of applying:

Step One: Positioning Yourself for Success

As an applicant, you have to make yourself appear to be as well rounded as possible. If, for example, you are very athletic and were hoping to be rewarded for your involvement in competitive sports, it is highly likely that, though you are deserving, other applicants may have more than one exceptional trait. You will have the best results if you can be involved more than the norm. Look for an extracurricular club to join. If nothing at your school appeals to you, get some people with a common interest together and find a teacher willing to act as your advisor and start a club of your own. This way you are not only a member of an extracurricular activity but you are also the founder and president of the club. By doing this, your application can emphasize initiative and leadership skills (two traits that are extremely important in the final decision-making process).

It is also a good idea to be involved outside of sports and school. Volunteering in your community can not only prove to be beneficial to your scholarship application but can also be very rewarding. Again, volunteer in a position that shows leadership or some other admirable quality. Picking up garbage at the town park will not win as many people over as working with children or seniors. If you live in a province that requires so many hours of community service to graduate from high school, be sure to greatly exceed that number. Also, do not limit yourself to one extracurricular or volunteering position—do as many as you can. These are not meant to be a punishment—if you join the right club, the right sport, or find the right volunteer position, you can have a lot of fun!

Finally, it is important that you have some sort of a part-time job. Review panels like to see that you are both involved and preparing for your future at the same time. Having a part-time job on top of everything else also shows good time management and can often lead to full-time summer employment while you are attending school. The income earned through the part-time job will also assist in paying for your education.

Step Two: Securing Solid References

Good references can be just as important as grades or involvement. References can be obtained through family, friends, part-time job managers/supervisors, school, and through community involvement. Keeping in mind that you are competing for scholarships, it is important that you give yourself any edge that you possibly can. This is why you should do your best to network and become acquainted with the senior management of any organizations you may be working with. If you are in any clubs at school, you should get to know the administration and try to get a reference from the principal or vice-principal (however, you have to make sure these people know you well enough to write really good letters of reference). The same rule can apply to any situation. Try to get a letter of reference from a manager rather than your immediate supervisor, and so on.

Most scholarships require letters of reference to come in envelopes with signatures across the seal of the letter. To be prepared, make sure you get your letters months before scholarship deadlines and get lots of extra copies signed and sealed.

Step Three: The Application

The purpose of the scholarship application is to highlight your strong points. Most applications ask for letters of reference and a transcript as well as ask questions about what you have done in the past few years. You will often find that the basic questions do not vary that much from one application to another. For example, every application will ask for an example of leadership and list of things you have been involved in. Because of this, you should start saving all of this type of information on your computer. Very quickly, you will accumulate a list of twenty answers or more and the time it will take you to fill out any application will be greatly reduced. Keep in mind: this is not a way of cutting corners. Try to answer all the questions with relevant and useful answers that can assist you in achieving your goal. Remember to emphasize all of your positive qualities, make sure your answers are well written (no spelling or grammar mistakes), and fill out as many applications as possible.

With the cost of post-secondary education being as high as it is, every dollar counts. This is why scholarships are so great. There are so many available in Canada, that if you are willing to invest some time researching and applying, you are almost guaranteed to find one that fits you. Remember, when looking at the big picture, this small investment in time can turn out to be a great investment in your future.

Learning to Save and Budget

When you leave home to go to a college or university, knowing how to save and budget will allow you to stretch your money much further. While you are young, it is important to hone this skill as much as you can as it is not only applicable to the next few years but also the rest of your life. If you intend on going away to school, the transition from living on your own can often be costly as you may find yourself overspending on the necessities, leaving yourself with less money for everything else. This section will provide tips on budgeting your weekly allowance as well as saving for larger expenses both expected and unexpected.

Saving Up

You should do your best to have your money for school expenses coming in consistently rather than in unpredictable boosts. Ideally, you will know exactly how much money you have to spend each week after any monthly bills or costs have been deducted. If you can figure this number out, you are then in a better position to plan ahead. Planning ahead can mean anything from "I want to go out to a concert with friends this Friday" to "I have to buy two new books for school next month." We do not always know when these expenses are coming, but it must be recognized that they will come. To be prepared, it is best to put away some portion of your allotted weekly amount of money into a savings account and then separate that into short- and long-term savings. For example, if you have $120 per week to spend, $20 could be saved. Of that, $10 could be saved for unexpected social outings and the other $10 could be put away for larger, one-time expenses such as having to buy furniture for an apartment or getting a new computer. As every person's needs and wants are different, how much money you should put away each week will vary. We stress the importance of planning ahead and expecting the unexpected.

The Weekly Budget

Once you know how much money you have at your disposal each week and how much you plan on saving, you can plan your budget much easier. When it comes to buying groceries and wanting to go out with friends, there are ways to maximize your money. When buying groceries, buy the cheapest essentials (milk, bread, sugar, flour, etc.). There are very few differences between name-brand and store-brand labels (no-name). You could also read local grocery-store flyers every week and try to buy the advertised specials. Most grocery stores pick items each week to sell at cost or just barely above cost to attract customers. Try planning meals around these specials and always make a weekly grocery list. Buying all of your groceries at once and sticking to a list will ensure that no money is wasted on unnecessary items. Shopping on an empty stomach is not recommended as you may buy items you don't really need such as snacks. Finally, compare prices at every grocery store in your area as there are usually differences in many staple items. (If there is a Costco or Sam's Club in your area, the price per gram of meat and seafood is considerably lower than the price in a normal grocery store.) You can also team up with other students to buy bulk items with the bulk savings and split the items up afterwards.

Here are a few tips on how to save money if you are the type of person who enjoys going out:

- Eating out: Instead of going to a restaurant, get some friends together and have each person prepare their favourite dish. You can make your own appetizers, desserts, and have your own drinks. The savings are quite considerable when you all prepare the meal as a group. In addition, you save on additional taxes and gratuities.

• Going to a movie: Most cinemas have a cheap-ticket night. Go then.

• Bar and club hopping: If you like this scene, you know how expensive it can be. To save money, we recommend, if you consume alcohol, do so in moderation and/or drink non-alcoholic beverages. Another tip: drink water or a soft drink in between alcoholic drinks.

With respect to living in residence or an apartment, this doesn't have to be a frugal situation. There are many ways to plan, budget, and save so that you enjoy yourself without spending a lot of money. Therefore, planning and budgeting in this respect can assist in paying for your post-secondary education.

Part-Time Jobs

For many post-secondary students, part-time jobs provide a steady income throughout the school year. In fact, as of 2004, approximately 40% of university students had part-time jobs. Whether the money is used for food, clothing, rent, utilities, or merely for everyday expenses, the financial benefits of working part-time should not be overlooked. In this section, we will look at many aspects of working part-time including:

• Is it right for you?
• Where should you look for a job?
• What can you expect?

Before you start making copies of your resumé, you should first determine whether a part-time job is right for you. Every student's financial situation is different, and there are various jobs that will cater to these special requirements. When you first consider looking for a part-time job, you must clearly define your goals. Are you looking for a couple shifts per week to increase your spending money or do you need a more consistent work schedule to pay for your fixed expenses? Though some may be lucky enough to find a career-related part-time job in their current field of study, we will assume that you are looking for any job that will provide you with a paycheque every two weeks.

Examples of typical part-time job opportunities include: retail sales, fast-food establishments, sit-down restaurants, movie theatres, grocery stores, convenience stores, office work, and tutoring. These opportunities offer different wages, schedules, duties, and responsibilities that you must be aware of.

A main aspect you must consider is your availability. In university, you usually have the freedom to set up your own class schedule. Once this is set, you can determine where you have spare time to work a few shifts. For example, if you finish class late everyday (around 5 or 6 p.m.), you may want to consider working in restaurants as opposed to retail stores. Most retail stores close at 9 p.m., so this would not leave you much time to put in a decent shift. Restaurants, on the other hand, will only start to get busy after your classes end and will usually stay open until around midnight. You would therefore have more opportunities for longer shifts. Keep in mind that even though some employers are more flexible with students' schedules, they still expect you to be able to put in a consistent amount of hours each week. By applying for the right type of job, you will make it easier to achieve your financial goals.

After you determine what type of job you're after, the next step is to find a company that is hiring. There are many places you can look, but the easiest way to find a job is by word of mouth. The more you let people know that you're looking for a job, the greater your chances that someone you know will offer you one or point you in the right direction. Many part-time jobs are earned through connections and often these jobs don't even get posted or advertised. It is very likely that you are already connected to someone who has a position to fill. By developing relationships and making it known that you are looking for employment, you should find it much easier to land your first part-time job.

For a more structured approach, you can try the more traditional method of newspaper classifieds. This method will provide many offers, but the challenge will be finding one that meets your criteria. School newspapers may prove to be more promising than local newspapers because they tend to be specifically targeted towards students who are looking to work while in school.

There are web sites that are gaining popularity with job seekers. This means, however, that there is stiff competition for the posted jobs since there is such a vast pool of potential applicants. If you have the patience, you may wish to try your luck with sites such as www.jobpostings.ca or www.workopolis.com. Your campus career centre may also be a useful resource in your job search and they are increasingly posting their job search engines online.

If you have a specific company in mind, you should definitely take a look at their web site as there are often instructions on how to apply online. Although, if you want to make a more personal application, a visit to the company will have a more significant impact and increase your chances of getting hired.

When you eventually get that part-time job, keep in mind that your primary occupation is still a student. The job will help you financially, but if it interferes too much with your school work, you may want to consider finding a new job or stop working altogether.

If you can only work about ten hours per week, at minimum wage that will leave you with a bimonthly paycheque of under $150 before taxes (this may vary depending on where you live). Although you will likely pay very little taxes as a student, you can fill out a TD1 form from your employer, which will instruct them to deduct as little as possible from your paycheque. You should still keep some disposable income aside and save or invest it in case you owe taxes at the end of the year, in which case you will have at least earned interest on the extra take-home pay as opposed to having it taken away at every paycheque. If your take-home pay is not worth the effort, you should seriously reconsider your situation. This may mean finding a better-paying job or working more hours. However, it will be very difficult to apply yourself to your school work if you end up working more than fifteen hours per week.

Another aspect to consider is how much your job is actually costing you. If you require a certain dress code or uniform that is not provided or that you do not currently own, you may be looking at spending a few hundred dollars just to get dressed for work. Also, travelling costs should be taken into account. Bus fare, gas, and/or parking all eat up part of your paycheque. The time spent travelling is also time wasted that could have been spent earning money. If you have to travel an hour each way to work a four-hour shift, chances are that the job isn't worth the hassle. When you factor in the fixed costs of going to work, you might even end up losing money. The less you have to travel, the more money you'll have to spend as you wish, so travelling expenses should not be overlooked.

Although everyone's work ethic is different and some may be able to handle more hours than others, remember why you started working in the first place. Part-time jobs can provide supplementary funds to get you through your post-secondary education. But unless you get through school successfully, you won't get the chance to start a full-time job, which is really the ultimate goal.

Registered Education Savings Plans (RESPs)

RESPs are a very popular form of funding a student's post-secondary education. (If you are currently a student, learning about RESPs may not be your priority at the moment but you may need to know this for your future.) An RESP is a contract set up between a subscriber and a promoter that is registered by the Canada Revenue Agency (CRA). Its purpose is to promote and facilitate the saving of funds for a beneficiary's post-secondary education. In general, the subscriber makes periodic payments to the promoter over many years. These funds are complemented by Canada Education Savings Grants (CESGs) provided by the Minister of Human Resources Development Canada. The funds accumulated in the RESP can then be paid back to the subscriber or beneficiary or through Educational Assistance Payments (EAPs) or Accumulated Income Payments (AIPs).

Anyone can enter into an RESP as a subscriber—even students themselves. Subscribers must provide the promoter with their social insurance number (SIN) before entering the plan. There is the possibility of having joint subscribers for those who enroll with a spouse or common-law partner. The beneficiary can be anyone who is under twenty-one years old and is a resident of Canada at the time of enrollment. The beneficiary's SIN must also be provided to the promoter. Under family RESPs, you may designate more than one beneficiary, but each must be related by blood or by adoption to the subscriber.

Unlike the contributions made to a Registered Retirement Savings Plan (RRSP), the contributions made to the RESP made by the subscriber are not tax deductible. However, they remain tax sheltered while they sit in the RESP over the years. If the subscriber eventually receives the payment at the closing of the RESP, he or she will not have to include the amount as income since this would be "double-counting" this amount as income. If the beneficiary receives the payment, they will have to include it in their income, but as students, they are usually in a very low tax bracket, which demonstrates the appeal of RESPs.

In addition to the subscriber's contributions, the Minister of Human Resources Development Canada will add a CESG equal to 20% of the annual contributions to a beneficiary's RESP up to an annual limit of $400. In other words, if a beneficiary's subscriber(s) contribute(s) at least $2,000 to their RESP in a given calendar year, the beneficiary will also receive a CESG of $400. CESGs, however, are only offered on contributions made by the end of the calendar year in which the beneficiary turns seventeen years old. So a beneficiary can receive up to eighteen of these CESGs in his or her lifetime for a total of $7,200. The program also offers a catch-up process: you can carry forward any unused grant room. You should contact the administrator (bank or financial planner) of your RESP for further explanation of this feature.

There are limits associated with the contributions to each beneficiary's RESP. There is an annual contribution limit of $4,000 and a lifetime contribution limit of $42,000. Keep in mind that these are limits per beneficiary, not per subscriber. Therefore, if a beneficiary has more than one RESP set up by multiple subscribers, these subscribers must be aware of the total contributions to the beneficiary so as not to exceed the limits.

Should a beneficiary's RESP contributions exceed the annual

limit of $4,000, the subscribers will have to pay a monthly tax of 1% on the amount exceeding the limit, proportional to their contribution share. This tax will have to be paid each month until the excess amount is withdrawn from the RESP. CESGs are not included in the calculation of the annual contribution limit, but any over-contributions (even after they are withdrawn) are included when calculating the lifetime contribution limit.

If the subscriber wishes to withdraw RESP contributions before maturity for non-educational purposes, the income will not be taxable. Any CESG earnings, however, will have to be refunded.

At the maturity of the RESP, the promoter can pay the RESP and CESG amounts to the beneficiary through EAPs to help pay for the costs of post-secondary education. This can only occur if the beneficiary is a full-time student in a qualifying educational program at a post-secondary educational institution or if the beneficiary can no longer attend school full-time due to medical or physical impairment. In order to qualify as an educational program, the student must spend at least ten hours per week for a minimum of three consecutive weeks on the course. The program will not qualify if it is taken at a time during which the student is receiving employment income (excluding part-time or temporary employment to finance studies) and the program is taken in connection with, or as part of, the student's employment. According to the Canada Revenue Agency, a post-secondary educational institution includes:

- A university, college, or other designated educational institution in Canada;
- An educational institution in Canada certified by the Minister of Human Resources Development Canada as offering non-credit courses that develop or improve skills in an occupation; and
- A university, college, or other educational institution outside Canada that has courses at the post-secondary school level, as long as the student is enrolled in a course that lasts at least thirteen consecutive weeks.

EAPs cannot exceed $5,000 until the student has completed thirteen consecutive weeks of the educational program. After this period, EAPs are unlimited, unless the student interrupts the program for thirteen consecutive weeks, in which case the $5,000 limit will be reapplied. This limit may be waived by the Minister of Human Resources Development Canada if tuition and related expenses in a certain program are far greater than normal.

If the beneficiary does not qualify for EAPs, has reached twenty-one years of age, or has died, the income earned in the RESP may be returned to the subscriber by Accumulated Income Payments (AIPs) if the subscriber is a Canadian resident. In order for AIPs to occur, the RESP must have been in place for at least ten years. AIPs are taxable according to the subscriber's marginal tax rate. This may be avoided by transferring the income to the subscriber's RRSP or spousal RRSP if possible. Otherwise, the income will also be subject to an additional 20% tax on AIPs.

RESPs are a useful tool for financing a student's post-secondary education. They are especially attractive due to the tax savings implications and the CESG benefits. With proper planning and management, RESPs can help provide students with the necessary funds for their education. If you need assistance calculating what you can and can't do within the RESP, we recommend you sit down with a financial planner to examine all your opportunities. Again, being well informed and planning ahead can alleviate many of the financial burdens now and later.

Line of Credit & Student Loans

RESPs are a great way of financing education for those who planned ahead. But what if you don't have an RESP set up for you? An alternative would be to apply for a line of credit or a student loan. Though all lines of credit are based upon the same principle, we will look at the line of credit for students offered by most financial institutions. We cover lines of credit in more detail in Chapter Six and student loans in Chapter Three.

A line of credit is a special type of loan whereby instead of borrowing the entire principal up front, you are provided with a credit limit and you can withdraw funds as needed. The limits are usually lower for undergraduate students and higher for post-graduate students. The key to a line of credit is that you only pay monthly interest on the amount you withdraw. So if you don't need the entire amount, you simply withdraw the portion you need and pay monthly interest on that amount instead of on the entire amount.

The interest rate charged for a student line of credit can be as low as the prime rate plus 1%. The prime rate is the rate that the bank offers to its best customers. Prime plus 1% is therefore an exceptionally low interest rate. This interest rate is a variable, floating rate, which means it will change from time to time when the financial institutions change their prime rate. (This usually takes place when the Bank of Canada changes the bank rate.) As of summer 2005, the prime rate at most financial institutions was 4.25%, and over the past five years this rate has been as low as 3.75% and as high as 7.75%.

With a student line of credit, you are only responsible for paying the outstanding monthly interest payments. If you don't make any withdrawals, you have nothing to pay. You can also avoid paying interest by repaying your withdrawal amounts every month. Any principal amounts that you withdraw are only due after you graduate and some financial institutions provide a grace period for repaying the principal. During this period, the financial institution allows you to continue paying interest. At that time, you will have the option of setting up a fixed payment schedule to pay off the line of credit. The fixed payment schedule will now include principal and interest payments combined.

A line of credit can provide you with the necessary financing without the hassle of regular loans. If you use it wisely, it is a very attractive way of borrowing funds and these funds are easily accessible at any time. You can withdraw from your line of credit at any bank branch, bank machine (ATM), by issuing cheques, and/or by telephone and Internet banking.

So, how do you set up a line of credit? First, you will need the following:

- Confirmation that you are enrolled at a Canadian post-secondary educational institution;
- An estimate of your education costs (including tuition, supplies, fees, accommodations, food, travel, etc.); and
- A list of your financial resources (including savings, bursaries, summer employment, etc.).

You will then meet with a credit specialist to assess your financial situation. Together, you will look at your financial needs and ability to repay. You may need to cover your line of credit with some personal assets (in which case, it would be considered a secured line of credit). If your credit history is not at the required level, you could use a co-signer who may help you secure the line. (Chapter Six reviews this in greater detail.) The line of credit is a very useful finance tool, but like all other debts, it should be managed prudently and wisely. You don't want to graduate with a large amount of debt and start your new career and life with a financial hangover.

There are many ways to access money for your post-secondary education and all of them involve some planning, budgeting, saving, or some form of debt. One of the most popular ways is through the student loan programs administered by the federal and provincial governments. In Chapter Three, we cover the student loan programs quite extensively. After you review all of your options such as loans, lines, RESPs, part-time work, savings, and any other format of financing such as family gifts, you should have a better chance of reaching your goal. As we have mentioned in earlier areas, the more informed you are, the easier it is to attain your goals.

Chapter Three
Student Loans

Introduction to Student Loans

Financing your post-secondary education can be a difficult and exhausting process. However, it is a very important step in achieving a rewarding and stress-free educational experience. Planning is very crucial when deciding your future, and getting all the facts can assist in this plan. Previous chapters focused on other aspects of financing, with some information on student loans. This chapter will focus exclusively on student loans. There are various levels of student loan coverage available to students from coast to coast. Depending on the province or territory of your residence, different plans of financing can be accessed. Regardless, if you are a student in need of financial aid, some form of government assistance is available depending on your eligibility.

There are some important decisions you should make prior to applying for a student loan. The two most important ones are choosing your institution and your program of study. The following pages will briefly illustrate the differences between a public and private post-secondary institution and between various fields of study.

Post-secondary education is a costly and time-consuming investment. Therefore, the process of planning beforehand is an extremely valuable one. After establishing your initial goals or reasons for attending a post-secondary institution, be it career or personal aspirations, you must decide on the program of study that will satisfy those immediate and long-term goals. Different universities offer different levels of student tuition, depending on the particular choice. While these may not vary significantly, it is important to know the true cost of education before applying.

There are also many levels of post-secondary education that you must choose from. These include:

- Universities (usually publicly funded, offering under-graduate programs that can last from three to five years and graduate programs that usually last for two years)
- Community colleges (funded both publicly and private-ly, offering diplomas with programs that last from one to three years)
- Technical schools (usually privately funded, offering cer-tificates and diplomas that last from one to two years and are usually targeted towards the current labour market)
- Private vocational schools (funded entirely through stu-dent tuition, offering diplomas that last from one to two years and provide job-specific training)

Rules of Engagement

In order to qualify and receive federal and provincial loan assistance, you must choose an institution that is specifically des-ignated by your local provincial or territorial student assistance office. The complete list of designated institutions both in Canada and internationally can be found on the following web site of Human Resources and Skills Development Canada: *http://www.rhdcc.gc.ca/asp/gateway.asp?hr=en/hip/cslp/ImportantLinks /02_il_MasterListIndex.shtml&hs=cxp.*

It is also possible to receive a full-time federal student loan to study in a post-secondary institution outside Canada. If the inter-national institution of your choice is listed as a designated institu-tion by Human Resources and Skills Development Canada at the above web site, all necessary forms must be obtained at your local provincial or territorial student assistance office. Contact informa-tion for all provincial and territorial student assistance offices is listed in the appendices.

Once you decide on the need for a student loan, here are the options available as well as the processes involved in obtaining the money:

Full-time students

A full-time student is defined as one that is enrolled in a minimum of 60% of a full course load (a student with permanent disabilities may enroll in 40% of a full-time load).

For residents of Newfoundland and Labrador, Prince Edward Island, Nova Scotia, New Brunswick, Manitoba, Alberta, British Columbia, and Yukon:

Apply for both the federal and provincial student loan program with one application form.

Repay each loan separately (federal loan through the National Student Loans Service Centre (NSLSC) and the provincial loan through a financial institution that was in charge of issuing it).

For residents of Ontario and Saskatchewan:

Apply for both the federal and provincial student loan program with one application form.

Repay both loans together through the National Student Loans Service Centre (NSLSC) due to a system called integrated student loans.

For residents of Quebec, Northwest Territories, and Nunavut:

Do not participate in the federal student loans program.

Only apply for the provincial or territorial student loan program.

Province or territory of residence is defined as the one in which a student has most recently lived for at least twelve consecutive months, excluding any time spent as a full-time student in a post-secondary institution.

Part-time students

A part-time student is defined as one that is enrolled in between 20% and 59% of a full course load (a student with permanent disabilities may enroll in between 20% and 39% of a full-time load).

For residents of all provinces and territories not eligible for a provincial or territorial student loan program:

Only apply for the federal student loan program.

Repay the loan through the National Student Loans Service Centre (NSLSC).

The Federal Loan Program

The federal student loan program is called the Canada Student Loans Program (CSLP). It was designed to provide accessible post-secondary education opportunities for students with financial need and to promote developing knowledge and skill-based career options for millions of Canadians. Created in 1964, the CSLP has since helped over 3.8 million Canadians realize their goals and dreams of post-secondary education and the subsequent participation in the Canadian economic and societal affairs. The running total of student loans provided by the CSLP since its creation is well over $16 billion. Every year, over three hundred fifty thousand students receive subsidized loans through the Canada Student Loans Program.

The CSLP is a product of close cooperation between the various provincial and federal governments. As mentioned earlier, the ten provinces and territories follow federal criteria in determining the eligibility and the amount of student loans issued, as well as designate eligible post-secondary institutions. While Quebec, Northwest Territories, and Nunavut do not directly participate in the CSLP, they receive alternative payments from the federal government to administer their own student assistance programs.

A newly designed feature of the CSLP is known simply as integration. The process of integration refers to the underlying desire within both federal and provincial governments to simplify the processes of application and repayment for student residents of their respective provinces or territories. Since August 2001, residents of Ontario and Saskatchewan have been able to take advantage of this simplified version of the combined federal and provincial student loan program. What does this mean?

- one application
- one need assessment
- one loan certificate
- one loan agreement form
- common repayment assistance measures
- one loan consolidation form and process
- one interest relief application

All of this boils down to the following: the student has one student debt and a single payment is required when repaying his/her student loan. This is very convenient and easier to manage.

The maximum amount that can be covered by the Canada Student Loan Program is 60% of assessed need up to a maximum of $165 per week. The provincial or territorial student loan program may provide up to 40% of your assessed need amount. Once your application (one or two depending on your province or territory of residence) is completed, your local student assistance office will notify you of the amount of student loan that you are eligible to receive.

To learn more about the Canada Student Loans Program visit their web site: *http://www.hrsdc.gc.ca/en/gateways/nav/top_nav/program/cslp.shtml*

Provincial Loan Programs

As mentioned earlier, provinces and territories offer different programs of financial assistance for students. Regardless of whether they participate in the CSLP or not, provincial and territorial governments in Canada are responsible for administering provincial loans, bursaries, and grants and, if applicable, federal loans, bursaries, and grants. In addition, provincial/territorial governments' duties are to:

- Provide students with application forms and student guides;
- Communicate with current and prospective students, as well as with various post-secondary institutions in matters concerning student loans;

- Assess financial need for each applicant utilizing federally established eligibility criteria;
- Calculate the amount of funding to be provided to each student via federal and provincial loans, bursaries, and grants;
- Review assessments; and
- Distribute bursary/grant money to students and post-secondary institutions.

While the Canada Student Loan Program is administered by provincial and territorial governments where it's applicable, Quebec, Northwest Territories, and Nunavut are not participants and administer their own student assistance programs. Some of the specific features of each program are outlined below:

Quebec
- Applicants must be Quebec residents (either Quebec-born or have parents that reside in Quebec);
- Students can apply for loans and/or bursaries from the provincial government;
- Maximum period of eligibility for a loan is the set duration of the program of study plus fifteen months (at up to $950 per month);
- Maximum period of eligibility for a bursary is the set duration of the program of study plus six months;
- Repayment commences six months after completion of studies (interest starts accruing immediately upon completion of studies).

Northwest Territories
- Applicants must be residents of the Northwest Territories;
- There are three categories of applicants: Northern indigenous Aboriginal residents, Northern residents schooled in NWT, and Northern residents not schooled in NWT;
- Students can apply for loans and/or grants;
- Grants do not have to be repaid and generally can be

used to cover travel and tuition expenses;
- Maximum period of eligibility for a loan is twenty semesters with a lifetime loan limit of $47,000;
- Repayment commences six months after completion of studies (interest starts accruing immediately upon completion of studies).

Nunavut
- Applicants must be residents of Nunavut;
- Students can apply for loans and/or grants;
- Grants do not have to be repaid and generally can be used to cover travel and tuition expenses;
- Lifetime loan limit of $36,000;
- Repayment commences six months after completion of studies (interest starts accruing immediately upon completion of studies).

For more information on each provincial and territorial student assistance program, refer to the appendices for a contact list.

Eligibility

All of the following requirements must be met in order to be eligible to apply for and receive assistance from the Canada Student Loans Program (CSLP):
You must:
- be a Canadian citizen, permanent resident, or a protected person (including convention refugee status);
- be a resident of province or territory that participates in the CSLP;
- demonstrate and provide documentation of financial need;
- enroll in a minimum 60% of a full course load (students with permanent disabilities may enroll in a minimum 40% of a full-time load);
- enroll in a post-secondary educational program of at least twelve weeks in length (within a period of fifteen consecutive weeks) at a designated institution;

• maintain a satisfactory academic record; and
• pass a credit check if you are twenty-two years of age or older and applying for a Canada Student Loan for the first time.

The term length of your student loan depends on the length of your program of study. Each student that meets all the criteria of the CSLP is eligible to receive financial assistance for the usual number of periods required to complete a particular program plus another period. For example, if you are enrolled in an undergraduate program that usually takes four years to complete, you will be eligible to receive federal student loans for a period of four years plus one extra year for a final total of five years. It is important to note that you continually demonstrate all the necessary criteria to qualify for a student loan to receive assistance in all subsequent years of study. Should your financial status change during the course of your study, your local provincial or territorial student assistance office must be notified and contacted for further information. Contact information for all provincial and territorial student assistance offices is listed in the appendices.

Ineligibility

Students may be ineligible for a loan for the following reasons:

• A previous default on a prior Canada Student Loan or provincial loan;
• If the student is under investigation for breaching terms and conditions of a loan previously received;
• Failing to meet academic-progress requirements;
• Significant variance in income reported to Canada Revenue Agency (CRA) and the amount indicated in the student's application; and/or
• Officials make the determination that the student does not demonstrate financial need.

Estimating Your Loan

The basic formula for calculating the size of your student loan is as follows:

ALLOWABLE COSTS* — RESOURCES = ASSESSED NEED

Allowable costs include:
• Tuition and student fees
• Books and other required materials
• Return transportation
• Living allowances
• Child allowances (if applicable)
• Day-care allowances (if applicable)

Resources include but are not limited to:
• Part- or full-time earnings and/or savings
• Earnings of your parents or spouses (if applicable)
• Scholarships and/or bursaries

*See Appendix B for an expense calculation chart

Student loans are designed to cover basic needs only. It is extremely important to report all relevant information to your local student assistance office when applying for a student loan; failure to do so may result in having to pay back some of the financial assistance received and even criminal prosecution. Honesty is the best policy here!

Applying for a Student Loan

Once you have figured out the rough amount of student loans (both federal and provincial) that you are eligible to receive, the following steps must be taken to complete the application process (student loan applications can be found on the various web sites listed in Appendix A):

1. Visit your local provincial or territorial student assistance office for a copy of an application. Often, these are also available at your high-school guidance counsellor's offices. Additionally, Nova Scotia, New Brunswick, Quebec, Ontario, Manitoba, Saskatchewan, Alberta, British Columbia, and Northwest Territories provide their stu-

dents with the opportunity to apply for and check the status of their student loan applications online. Contact information for these provincial and territorial student assistance offices is listed in the appendices.

2. After carefully reviewing all items on the application form, fill it out using information that is correct and accurate to the best of your knowledge. This process may take some time, but it will go a long way to ensuring that you get the financial assistance that you require. If the local student assistance office is unsatisfied with your application, it may be returned to you or rejected altogether. Therefore, providing it with the most up-to-date information is of utmost importance.

3. Submit your application form either online or to your local student assistance office. Here are some helpful hints when submitting your application:
• Ensure you have your social insurance card with you;
• Bring two other pieces of identification (ID) just in case your particular office requires multiple pieces of ID, preferably a photo ID such as a driver's licence. (A health card may not be considered valid ID);
• Bring a void cheque because the money will either be directly deposited to your account or you will be sent the funds via a cheque. The account deposit is the most convenient setup;
• Call your student services building and ask them if they require any other documents from you. Don't be afraid to ask questions.

4. Deadlines for submission vary from province to province and year to year. It is your responsibility to submit your application on time. Otherwise, it will not be processed and you may lose out on a year of much-needed financial assistance.

5. Should you be approved for a student loan, your local student assistance office will mail you a letter of assessment, a certificate of eligibility, and a loan agreement. This should take place within four to six weeks of filing the application.

6. Take your certificate of eligibility to the post-secondary institution for completion.

7. After the certificate of eligibility is completed, you must sign it along with the loan agreement. Once again, accuracy and completing all required information is very important, as incomplete forms will not be processed.

8. Mail your completed documents to the National Student Loan Service Centre (NSLSC) via Canada Post within thirty days of them being signed by the post-secondary institution and before the end of the month of the period of study end-date that is indicated on your certificate of eligibility. You must deliver these documents in person to the closest Canada Post outlet. Valid photo ID will be required at that time. Do not forget to keep copies for your personal records as well as a receipt from Canada Post.

9. Your student loan can be directly deposited into your account if you provide a void cheque along with your loan documents. Funds will be deposited into your account within a week of the disbursement date on your certificate of eligibility or within a week of the documents being received by the NSLSC, whichever is later. If you do not provide a void cheque along with your documents, funds will be mailed to you at an address indicated on your loan documents. This would happen within two weeks of the disbursement date on your certificate of eligibility or within two weeks of the documents being received by the NSLSC, whichever is later. The disbursement date is defined as within a week of your period of study start-date.

10. Should your financial situation change any time during the school year or in between school years, your local student assistance office must be immediately notified of this change. This is to avoid future overpayments of student loans issued in your name. Your local student assistance office will let you know if and when your eligibility status or the amount of student loans that you are eligible for changes.

11. In order to avoid abuse of the loan system, the government regularly audits random files. If your file is selected for auditing, you will be asked to provide the following documents:
• copies of income tax returns
• T4 slips
• bank statements
• rent receipts
• letters from employers regarding your earnings
• receipts for tuition, books, and related materials
• child-care receipts (if applicable)
• separation/divorce agreements (if applicable)

As such, it is a good idea to keep track of your expenses at all time and retain documentation (receipts) to support your file information. If you do not respond to an audit request, your loan will be cancelled and future government assistance may be in jeopardy.

Maintaining Your Student Loan

After receiving your money, one safe option to manage your money is to keep it in a savings account. The interest earned in these accounts is minimal; however, savings accounts will discipline you to manage that money strictly for educational purposes because they typically charge a high fee for withdrawals. For example, TD Canada Trust has one type of savings account known as a guaranteed investment account. This account will yield 2% interest if the balance is maintained over $5,000. Again, the interest earned would then only be $100 for the year. However, keeping the money in this type of account would be a safe decision because you are allowed one free transaction a month, and after that, there is a charge of $5 per transaction. This fee will act as a barrier to any impulsive, unnecessary spending.

Different banks have different rates so if you are keen on earning interest on your money, you need to explore your various options. There are some bank accounts that pay reasonable interest rates, even equivalent to investments like guaranteed investment certificates (GICs) and savings bonds. According to www.canlearn.ca, some online banks, for example, are now paying interest in the 4% to 5% range (as of summer 2005). Internet banking and telephone banking are increasingly becoming popular methods for transactions. Considering that 98% of students have access to the Internet, managing your money online is quick and hassle-free. The added bonus with some of these accounts is that they also allow you no-fee transactions at the same time that your money is hard at work earning interest. And just like the bricks-and-mortar banks, your earnings are insured up to $60,000. To be on the safe side, you should verify that they are insured through the Canada Deposit Insurance Corporation (CDIC).

Once you have been approved for a student loan from the respective government's loan program, it is important to remember that you have to fulfill certain responsibilities in order to continue to receive it in your future years of study. In addition, you don't have to make any payments to the NSLSC until six months after your graduation, as long as you maintain your valid status within the Canada Student Loans Program and/or your provincial or territorial student assistance program. The responsibilities mentioned above include:

• Reapplying and providing proof of financial need each year that funding is needed;
• Relaying changes in your address, name, marital status, financial status, or student status to the NSLSC and to your provincial/territorial student assistance office; and
• Providing the NSLSC with proof of yearly full-time

enrollment in a designated institution by a certain deadline (even if you are not reapplying for a loan, this allows you to repay the amount already borrowed while you remain in school interest-free).

For students who are reapplying for a loan:

• Send your new certificate of eligibility to the NSLSC within six months of the period of study end-date (PSED) indicated on previous year's certificate of eligibility.
• Contact your provincial/territorial student assistance office to maintain your interest-free status on the provincial/territorial portion of your loan.

For students who are not reapplying for a loan (but are still in school):

• Fill out a copy of confirmation of enrollment form, which can be obtained at the NSLSC or your financial or post-secondary institution.
• Send this form to the NSLSC or your financial institution within six months of your last PSED indicated on the previous year's certificate of eligibility.

Repaying Your Loan

Having maintained your interest-free status throughout your enrollment, you will have to start repaying your loan and all the interest that accumulates in your account when you leave or graduate from school. A student loan is a serious financial obligation and, as such, must be entered into with a serious frame of mind and repaid in a fashion indicated in your student loan repayment form.

You will have six months after completing your studies (whether you graduate or not) until you have to make your first payment to the National Student Loans Service Centre (NSLSC), though interest will start to accumulate in the first month after study completion. This is what's generally referred to as the "six-month grace period." It is the government's way of allowing students time to seek and find appropriate employment in their respective fields of study. However, if you want to avoid paying extra interest that will be accrued in these six months, you can start making payments against the principal amount of your loan as soon as your studies are complete.

Interest Rates on Your Loan

When completing your repayment form, you will be asked to choose between two options concerning interest rates: the fixed option and the floating option.

The fixed option entails a repayment of:
PRINCIPAL AMOUNT + 5% INTEREST (permanent rate for the entire repayment)

The floating option entails a repayment of:
PRINCIPAL AMOUNT + 2.5% INTEREST (current rate that may change in the future; you retain the choice to switch to the fixed-rate option at any time)

Repaying Your Loan Easier and Faster

1. Completing a consolidated student loan repayment agreement is an important first step to keeping track of the repayment process. This agreement will consolidate the loans you've received over the years from the NSLSC into one loan and set the terms of your repayment schedule. On this consolidation agreement, you will choose your preferred option of interest-rate accumulation. After you forward it to the NSLSC, you will get it back with the information that will include the full amount of the loan, when your first payment is due, the number and frequency of your payments, and the amount of each payment. You must send the consolidation agreement to the NSLSC within six months of the completion of your studies.

2. With a pre-authorized payment plan, the NSLSC will automatically withdraw money from your bank account to

follow the repayment schedule. While normally withdrawn on the last day of each month, this can be changed according to your own needs. We recommend you set this up to coincide with your cash flow. If you want to take advantage of this option, send a completed form to the NSLSC along with a void cheque.

3. If you want to minimize the amount of interest that you will pay on the principal amount of your loan, making lump-sum payments while still in school or during the six-month grace period is the best way to accomplish that goal. At any of the above mentioned times and also at any time during the repayment schedule, you can complete a one-time debit form outlining the amount you wish to repay immediately. If you want to take advantage of this option, send a completed form to the NSLSC along with a void cheque.

Defaults and Bankruptcies

It is of utmost importance that you do not default on your student loan, as the Government of Canada will pursue various legal (using a private collection agency) and financial (notifying a credit agency) avenues against you. This may result in the seizing of your personal property and/or the downgrading of your credit rating. A poor credit rating fresh out of school is not a good way to start your career. Be careful, as many firms require a credit check before they hire you, especially for jobs in financial institutions.

You cannot avoid repaying your student loan by declaring bankruptcy for a period of ten years following the completion of your studies. Consequently, you must negotiate favourable repayment terms. You should schedule with the NSLSC and make sure that all regular payments are submitted on time and in appropriate amounts. Remember to plan ahead!

Steering Away from Debt: Options in Repaying Your Student Loan

Repaying your loan can be a significant burden, especially when you're fresh out of university and you haven't found your ideal job yet. Here are some options that you might consider in helping manage the repaying of your loans.

Federal Interest Relief

The interest that accumulates at the end of your study period is a considerable amount. The Canadian government will pay the interest on full- and part-time Canada Student Loans on behalf of people who have run into financial difficulties. If employment cannot be found or if a person has medical circumstances such as a temporary disability, the Government of Canada will cover the interest for a period of up to thirty months. To maintain that the interest be alleviated, borrowers must re-apply every six months. Also, during this interest-free period, applicants are not obligated to make payments on the principal amounts of the loans. The Federal Interest Relief Program is administered by the bank or the NSLSC with the Canadian Student Loan account. Although the maximum designated period of the interest relief is thirty months, the bank or the NSLSC may approve extending the interest-relief period from thirty months to fifty-four months. In order to obtain this status, the student must be a post-secondary graduate for no more than five years. The eligibility criteria is as follows:

The borrower must:

1. Be a resident of Canada;

2. Have not been granted, including the period being applied for, more than thirty months of special interest-free periods under this plan;

3. Have at least one of the following circumstances apply:
• Unemployed (unemployed means, in the four weeks immediately prior to application, the debtor had worked eighty hours or less), available for work, and actively seeking employment of more than twenty hours per week;
• Incapable of working due to a temporary disability or illness. The condition must be substantiated by documentation from a doctor indicating the nature of the illness or disability and probable duration;

• Have a family income such that the repayment of Canada Student Loans/BC Student Loans could cause exceptional financial hardship.

Federal Debt Reduction

Another option that you can apply for if you experience immense difficulty repaying your student loan is federal debt reduction. Students who have fully utilized the Interest Relief Program or those who have been out of post-secondary studies for at least five years may qualify for debt reduction. Interest relief in conjunction with the possibility of the Federal Debt Reduction Program is intended to reduce the Canada Student Loan principal to a more affordable amount. The eligibility criteria is as follows:

• The borrower must have exhausted all available interest relief.
• The borrower must have a repayment period of at least fifteen years.
• Sixty months (five years) must have passed since the borrower's most recent period of study end-date (PESD).
• The borrower's loan must be in good standing.
• The borrower must demonstrate that he/she has an income stream to support the post-reduction payment (the ability to pay will be based on family income).

Application forms for the Federal Debt Reduction Program can be obtained through the National Student Loan Service Centre.

Loan Forgiveness Programs

Have you ever even heard of a loan forgiveness program? Well, if you haven't, then this option might extensively help you out of debt. Each province has different programs established to assist students who are just out of college or university. Several provincial governments have recognized the increasing need for skilled, trained, and educated professionals. In order for people to become prominent members of society, loan forgiveness programs are established and vary from province to province. Assessing whether you are eligible for this program means that a portion of your debt can be forgiven. Detailed information regarding the criteria to apply for each program within each province can be obtained through contacting the student assistance office. The following are the loan forgiveness programs for British Columbia and Ontario to give you a general idea of what the options might resemble.

BC Loan Forgiveness Program

This program has been designed to provide British Columbia Student Loan (BCSL) forgiveness to students graduating from accredited post-secondary educational institutions who agree to practice full-time, part-time, or casual in a publicly funded facility in an underserved area of British Columbia for three years.

Graduates from accredited schools in nursing (including licensed practical nursing) and from medical, midwifery, and pharmacy schools who began their final year of study on or after August 1, 2000, will have all outstanding BCSL debt forgiven at a rate of 33% per year of practice.

Students graduating on or after December 1, 2004, in the professions of speech language pathology, occupational therapy, audiology, and physiotherapy who will be working with children in underserved communities, will have all outstanding BCSL debt forgiven at a rate of 33% per year of practice.

Ontario Loan Forgiveness Program

The Ontario Loan Forgiveness Program has been replaced by the Ontario Student Opportunity Grant. The former Ontario Student Assistance Program (OSAP) will still continue for students who obtained loans issued from the 1993–94 academic year to the 1997–98 academic year. The Ontario Student Opportunity Grant, beginning in the 1998–99 academic year, is available to help students reduce the annual amount of their Canada-Ontario Integrated Student Loan. This program is a valuable option for people who are struggling to pay back their student loans because the program limits a student's repayable debt to $7,000 for a two-term academic year and $10,500 for a three-term academic year. It is available at the end of each of your academic years, and thus for students who have borrowed a vast amount from the Canada-Ontario student loan, this program can help reduce your debt. The loan forgiveness level is based on the number of terms in your study period.

Here is a chart of how the amounts were determined in Ontario in the past:

Total number of terms	Loan forgiveness levels *prior* to 1997-98	1997-98 loan forgiveness levels
1 term	not available	not available
2 terms	$6,000	$7,000
3 terms	$9,000	$10,500
4 terms	$12,000	$14,000
5 terms	$15,000	$17,500
6 terms	$18,000	$21,000
7 terms	$21,000	$24,500
8 terms	$24,000	$28,000
	For each additional term add $3,000	For each additional add $3,500

Source: *www.osap.gov.on.ca*

Other Conditions of Loan Forgiveness Programs

As we can see from the Ontario and British Columbia loan forgiveness programs, the two have different criteria in terms of who qualify. While British Columbia uses this program to draw people to work in public facilities in the underserved areas of BC, the loan forgiveness program in Ontario does not have these criteria. Other provinces might also have a minimum amount of debt required before you can qualify for a loan forgiveness program. For example, the Alberta Student Loan Relief Program (*http://www.aved. gov.bc.ca/studentservices*) requires that the minimum debt levels for students graduating in the 2003–2004 academic year be as follows to qualify:

- Private vocational schools (per four-month semester): $2,500
- Diploma program (2 x eight-month year): $10,000
- Degree program (4 x eight-month year): $20,000
- Master's program: $30,000
- PhD program: $35,000
- Veterinary Medicine, Chiropractic Study, Optometry: $40,000
- Law, MBA: $37,500
- Medicine: $55,000
- Dentistry: $67,500

The loan forgiveness programs provide people with assistance in repaying the large sums that they borrowed as a student. For students who had no other way of financing their education except for obtaining a significant debt, loan forgiveness is one of those benefits that Canada offers, yet, surprisingly, some people are unaware that this program exists at all. Thus, taking the time to research and explore all your options can save you thousands of dollars.

Chapter Four
Accommodation

Unlike their American counterparts, Canadian colleges and universities offer a more challenging yet motivating endeavour for students in terms of living accommodations. Although many universities offer residency for first-year students, the years after first year may entail that students move into their own residential space. In Canada, there is a trend of living off campus after the first year, and some schools do not even offer residence after this time (i.e. McGill University in Montreal). Students will need to understand what residential services their chosen college or university offers and then see what the norm is among students at the chosen institution. Not all students will decide to live away from home while attending post-secondary school, so it is important to look at the issues surrounding staying at home as well. The pros and cons of this situation are very important to consider. One important factor is transportation because it can be as costly as living away from home!

Moving out on one's own, choosing an apartment or residence, finding furniture, and adapting to a new lifestyle are all parts of the general college/university experience, turning students into responsible and aware individuals when the comfort of home is no longer an option. The notion of having to manage all of life's challenges at once can seem overwhelming at first but proper preparation and planning will enable students to make this transition a worthwhile learning experience. Through proper planning, the burden of expense issues will decrease, allowing college life to become an agreeable and fun undertaking. An organized student will be able to focus on the essential parts of their higher education and any other experiences they deem important. The years at college and university are a time for learning, and in this vital stage of life, more stress is the last thing any young person needs.

Nonetheless, no matter how vital these steps may be, human nature prevails as students rest on their laurels. If you make the mistake of being idle, you risk ending up in situations you would rather never have to experience. Imagine having the annoying guy from residence become your first roommate because all your friends found apartments together; or having an apartment so far from campus you have to wake up three hours before class just to be on time; or being forced to settle for the only available apartment, which is, unfortunately, located atop the loudest nightspot in town. All these situations have occurred to students across Canada, and will continue to take place, unless individuals prepare themselves and structure what they want to do in advance. We cannot stress enough the importance of how being ahead of the game will make your whole college or university experience better: trust us. Planning is the essence of making this happen.

We will now review the following: campus life, living at home, living on campus and living off campus, apartment responsibilities and considerations, and a new lifestyle. We will provide vital information to guide students on how to find the ideal location and what steps should be taken to make the search as quick and organized as possible. We will also offer tips that many students only come to learn after a disaster or from older peers. Therefore, take this information as concrete and useful advice to make your transition smooth and simple.

Campus Life

While aspects such as reputation and cost are important considerations for students, if you don't fit into the overall environment of a school, your post-secondary years will not only be painful on your wallet but also to your mental health. Choosing a school based on its compatibility with your personality and attitude is equally as important if you want to enjoy and benefit from the entire experience. There is really only one way to determine whether a school is right for you and that is to visit the campus. To make the process a little bit easier, ask yourself these simple questions at the beginning:

1. Do I want to live at home while attending college or university?
2. Do I want to live in a large city while attending college or university or would I rather live in a small town?
3. Do I want to go to a large school with fairly large class sizes or would I prefer a small school where I will get a little more individualized attention?

Based upon your responses to these questions, you will have a fairly good overview of the type of school and its location that is most likely to appeal to you. If you prefer to live in a large urban environment such as Toronto, Montreal, or Vancouver with their multicultural atmospheres and endless amounts of restaurants and clubs, these tend to be the places with the largest schools in the country with twenty thousand or more undergraduate students. However, smaller schools are also available, such as Ryerson University in Toronto and Simon Fraser University in Vancouver. Smaller towns and cities are where you typically find smaller universities, where much of the town's culture and spirit tend to revolve around the school and where you generally receive greater amounts of one-on-one attention from professors and advisors.

Most schools hold an "open house," usually sometime in February or March, where you can take a guided tour of the school and its facilities as well as talk to professors and students. This is the perfect opportunity to get to know a school, and if the open house is held during March break, you ought to think twice about a vacation and seriously consider visiting any university you have applied to and been accepted at. If you cannot visit schools during their open houses, there are other opportunities to check them out. Almost every school has a welcome centre, or some derivation of the title, where you can phone ahead of time and arrange to take a guided tour given by a student, and you may even be able to sit in on a lecture or two as well. In short, the ball is truly in your court and you should make every effort to visit the schools you are applying to. Most welcome centres try to make such visits as painless for potential students as possible. You are, after all, a potential customer for the school and they are not going to shrug you off. Not getting to know a school as best as you can before attending it may not only affect your academic and social life, if you find out the hard way that you made the wrong choice, it can be costly to switch schools later on.

Living at Home

The first option to consider is living at home while attending a post-secondary educational institute. But for many prospective students, this may not even be an option to consider, depending on how far away the school you're going to attend is from your home. However, provided that your program of choice is offered at a local school, it is worth considering living at home rather than going to some other school even if the tuition is higher locally. This is because living at home is basically free.

Living at home is by far the cheapest alternative and requires practically no effort in comparison to finding other accommodations. You do not have to worry about paying rent, going grocery shopping, and paying bills. These expenses add up very quickly and often amount to more than the yearly tuition fees to attend college or university. Therefore, if finances are an issue, living at home can greatly ease the stress of coming up with the money needed for your studies. For these reasons, living at home may seem like a "no-brainer," but, in fact, it can be just as complicated as the other options. It might be impossible in some cases if the program you wish to attend is not offered at any local schools or it might even be that there are no schools close by and that you must attend a school away from home.

Implications of Living at Home

Living at home has many other implications beyond the impact on finances. First, there is the question of your relationships with family members. For some, university is the chance to leave home and finally be free, while for others, leaving the safety of their parents' house gives them nightmares. It's important to think about the state of family relationships when making the decision of living at home or going away; you'll be either living with these people or living away from them for the next three or four years. This can have a huge impact on your performance in school if you cannot stand to live at home anymore or if your living away from home causes you to miss your family too much. Sit down and think about how you feel about your family and how you picture living with them for the next few years. It might also be a good idea to talk to your parents and ask them if they are expecting you to move out or if they're okay with you living with them through your college or university years.

Advantages of Living at Home

Living at home definitely has its advantages over living in your own apartment or in residence. As mentioned previously, it's by far the cheapest option for your choice of accommodation during the next few years of your life. When comparing the costs of living on your own versus staying at home, remember that if you stay at home, not only will you avoid paying rent but you'll also save by not having to buy furniture. In addition, your parents will most likely pay all the bills and your living expenses such as the electricity, gas, water, cable, Internet, and phone bills, and your groceries as well.

Secondly, you get to avoid the time and effort—and not to mention the headaches—associated with trying to find an apartment or applying for space in residence. Another benefit of living at home is that, in most cases, your parents will end up doing most of the cooking as well as a lot of other household tasks. University and college workloads can be quite overwhelming for many new students. Add to that the extra responsibilities of having to cook, clean, and pay bills, and the stress can be agonizing.

Another advantage of living at home is that you get to keep seeing your friends and you can continue whatever routine you have now. Compared to having to make new friends all over again while going to a new school and also having to worry about your finances, it is undeniably a boon to have a well-established support network of friends. Of course, you might want to ask your friends where they are going to school as it is possible, though unlikely, for you to find yourself friendless when all of them decide to go to a college or university away from your hometown. The point still stands, though, that living at home offers you stability and familiarity, not only with your friends and family but also through simply knowing your surroundings. This can help alleviate the stress of going to school during your first year and also make it much easier for you to find a job if you need one since all of your contacts are most likely in your hometown.

Disadvantages of Living at Home

To contrast all this, staying at home is not without drawbacks. First of all, touching on transportation, you will need to spend a significant amount of time every day going to school and coming back. It can easily take over an hour of your time to travel back and forth each day, and that's basically time wasted versus simply walking across the street to go to school if you live in an apartment nearby. Even though it's the cheapest way to go, living at home can have its disadvantages. For instance, there can be numerous distractions if you stay at home while studying, especially if you have a large family or younger siblings. Also, your studies will most certainly involve a great deal of teamwork, such as group assignments and projects or working in study groups. As a result, you'll probably end up having to commute to school on weekends and evenings, and the extra trips, by private or public transport, can really take their toll on you, leaving you both physically and mentally tired.

There are two major disadvantages of living at home. First, it becomes very easy to just go to class and come back home while missing out on student life. Second, you're not gaining any of the valuable living experience and independence you get from living away from home. As was mentioned, there is a lot more to college and university than academia and it is very important to get involved in student life. Not only does it make for great character building but also, when you have your degree and are looking for your first job, employers will look at what kind of extracurricular activities you were involved in to decide whether to hire you or not. If you live at home, it might be harder to get involved for many reasons. First, you might have to travel to school if the activity isn't right before or after one of your classes. Also, people who live near school all know one another by being neighbours and living on campus, so they tend to form a sort of clique. Finally, if you live at home, it is very likely that you will have all sorts of obligations outside of school and these can come into conflict with activities you would like to get involved in. Obviously, these are not insurmountable problems but they may hamper your ability to get involved as much as you would if you were living on campus.

As a prospective student, you've obviously decided to dedicate the next few years of your life to learning new skills and increasing your knowledge. There are, however, some things that simply aren't taught in a classroom. In fact, moving out on your own is probably one of the best ways to learn how to be autonomous and develop organizational skills. Going to college or university is often seen as a chance to become independent—to spread your wings and fly on your own so to speak. If you live at home, the proverbial nest, you will be passing on that opportunity to live on your own. Sure your parents will be taking care of you and you will have less stress by not having responsibilities such as food, laundry, and rent, but you will eventually have to shoulder these responsibilities. Going to a post-secondary school is a good time to do this since you have relatively few other responsibilities. Moreover, you may associate college and university with excitement, freedom, and becoming an adult. As a result, you may want to take the big jump and move out on your own even though you live close to the school you've chosen to attend. On the other hand, post-secondary education is getting more and more expensive and it might be more rational to cut back on such a big expense, if possible.

Although moving out on your own is definitely a very appealing idea, if you're lucky enough to have the choice of staying at home while going to school, you really need to look at this option in an objective fashion. So only after weighing the pros and cons of living at home while attending a post-secondary institution and determining how much you can afford to spend on your accommodations should you make a decision on whether to stay at home or move out.

Living at home offers some definite financial advantages over living on your own or in a school residence. These financial advantages can be overstated, however, so it is important to sit down and figure out just how much you will save (or how much more you will pay) by living at home. Moreover, choosing to live at home has implications beyond finances, namely on your relationship with family and friends and also in terms of opportunities for involvement in student life and gaining some independence. It is therefore important to look beyond the numbers and think about these other items. Living at home might save you some money, but is it worth the missed opportunities?

Transportation

Living at home is not completely free. One of the expenses that you will incur when living at home is transportation. Depending on how far away your school of choice is, you may have to pay for public transportation or own a car. To determine if staying at home is the right choice of accommodation for you, the first thing you should consider is how long it will take you to get to the school of choice from home every day and how you plan on getting there. You need to know if public transportation is available on a regular basis, or, if you plan on driving a car, if you will be required to commute during rush hour. Is traffic really dense or light? These factors can make a huge difference in your daily commute time, so you should try driving to the institution from your home during peak traffic hours to determine your daily travel time.

Public Transportation

If your hometown has a good public transportation service, that is to say relatively reliable with frequent stops, it's definitely an option you should look into for several reasons. First, the most obvious advantage, as compared to running an automobile, is that it's a lot cheaper, and there is usually a considerable reduction of the cost of a bus/train/subway pass for students, which can be very appealing. Furthermore, it's considerably more environmentally friendly than commuting by car.

Public transportation varies widely depending on where you live, both in cost and in quality of service. For example, a monthly student pass in Montreal costs $32.50, while in Toronto it costs $83.25. Moreover, public transportation in large cities such as Toronto, Montreal, and Vancouver is very reliable with hundreds of bus routes and frequent buses making it easy to get to school no matter where you live in the city. On the other hand, the buses in smaller cities may pass very infrequently and simply getting to school using public transportation can be a long and painful journey. It is therefore important to check how much public transportation in your area costs and whether or not a convenient route runs between your house and your school. Taking public transportation is a lot less stressful than driving in heavy traffic, and the ride goes by quickly as you can pass the time reading or playing portable video games, which you can't do when your hands are tied up at the wheel of a car. As noted earlier, the biggest disadvantage of public transportation, in most cases, is that it's very time-consuming in comparison to having your own vehicle. So, as we suggested with the option of commuting by car, use the public transportation system to travel to your future school from home in order to get an idea of how long your daily commute time will be.

Commuting by Automobile

The other choice is to commute to school by car. If you live outside of the area served by public transportation or if it is not convenient to take public transportation to go to school, this may be your only option and a costly one at that. Commuting by car is certainly more appealing than public transport—there's no waiting in the cold for buses, it's private, more comfortable, and usually a lot faster—but it is also much more expensive and, in some cases, even more expensive than living away from home. So if you don't already have a vehicle at your disposal, it's important to think about how much owning your own car really costs.

The initial cost of owning an automobile includes buying the car and paying interest if you finance the purchase with a loan. Additional costs include paying insurance, car registration fees, fuel, parking (which increases when the campus is located in a metropolitan area), service and maintenance costs, and, in some provinces, yearly vehicle inspections.

First, there is the cost of simply owning the car, be it buying or leasing it, which may not seem like much compared to renting an apartment, but many other bills come along with owning a car. Then there is the cost of gas; depending on how far your home is from school and how fuel efficient your car is, this can range widely and cost upwards of a hundred dollars a month. Furthermore, there is the cost of insurance, which also varies widely depending on what type of car you drive and whether you are male or female. Also, you must consider the cost of repairs to keep the car in good running order, which, again, varies depending on the make and model of your car. Finally, there is parking.

Parking is something we don't give a lot of thought to, but it can add up to a very sizable amount each month depending on where you live. Your school might have its own parking lot, which may or may not be free. If not, then you will have to park on the street or rely on paying parking lots. It is extremely important that you figure out how much parking will cost you every month if you are considering driving to school every day, especially if you live in a large city where parking can easily cost hundreds of dollars per month. If you live in a smaller city, parking near your school may be free, so driving to school becomes a more reasonable proposition.

Another consideration to keep in mind when contemplating driving to and from school in Canada is the climate. Snow and ice in the winter slows traffic down and is the cause of many accidents every year, and is even more dangerous if you have to travel on isolated roads. Therefore, you'll have to invest in a set of good winter tires, which can easily cost several hundred dollars.

You should most certainly consider the possibility of carpooling. Try picking classes so that your schedule coincides with that of a family member, friend, or classmate who could then drive you to and from school without having to make several extra trips.

Once you have determined how you'll be getting to school every day and how long the daily commute will be, ask yourself if the amount of commute time you'll be spending is acceptable to you. Note that the bus or car ride, if avoided, could be time used to study or work, and that the money forgone from this lost time should be calculated as an expense of living at home.

To figure out the monthly cost of owning a car, simply follow these steps:

1. If you are buying a car, divide the price by the number of months you will be attending university (including summer). If you are leasing it, you already know the monthly payment.

2. Add the monthly insurance premium for the car.

3. Estimate how much gas will cost by multiplying the distance between your home and school by the gas mileage of your car, then multiply this result by the price of gas, then multiply the total by forty as this is the number of times you will have to drive to school and back home every month. Add this final number to the total.

4. Find a reasonable estimate for the yearly cost* of repairs for your car and divide it by twelve then add it to the total.

5. Find out how much parking will cost you each month and add this number to the total.

*Please note that it is important to calculate the monthly cost of owning your car as if you were going to school twelve months a year. This is for comparison purposes as, should you choose to rent an apartment, you will have to pay rent for twelve months even if you are not living there during the summer.

Depending on the type of car, the grand total can be very surprising and quite close to the monthly rent for an apartment close to school. Of course, having your own car has its share of advantages including those beyond simply driving to school, so it is worthwhile to take into consideration.

Living On Campus

Unlike ten or fifteen years ago, many colleges and universities in Canada have a diversified selection of residential choices. Most offer the option of a traditional dormitory residence, where you share a room with someone and communal bathrooms are found on each floor. However, in recent years, non-traditional forms of residence accommodations have developed including apartment-style residences. In this type of residence, there are two or three people in each apartment—each person with their own room or perhaps sharing a room—and all share a common kitchen, living area, and bathroom. Some schools also offer residential housing in homes the school owns close to campus, again where you would either have your own room or would share a room, and then everyone would share a common area, kitchen, and bathroom. Check with the school that you are applying to and see if they offer these residence options because they are great alternatives to traditional dormitory living.

Besides just the amenities, one should consider the cost of each type of residential option, for as you can probably guess, living in residence is not cheap. On average, a double room can cost anywhere from $2,700 to $3,400 per year and a single room from $3,100 to $3,900 per year. Furthermore, non-traditional residences may in some cases be cheaper than traditional dormitory residences, while in other instances, they may be more expensive.

Be advised that in some cases, these non-traditional residences may not be right next to the school and may require you to take public transit to get to class, which will add an additional transportation cost to your budget. Be sure to check the details with the college or university because this can vary from school to school. The main reason why the non-traditional residences may be cheaper is that they tend not to offer a meal plan since they are equipped with kitchens so students can cook for themselves. The average meal plan can cost from $1,900 to $3,500 per year, and the food may not always have that home-cooked taste and can lack variety from week to week. If you're a good cook or are interested in becoming one, opting out of the meal plan is an easy way to shave $2,000 to $3,000 off your tuition. Also, some meal plans may only cover weekday meals, leaving students to pay for their own meals during the weekend.

If you are concerned about residences being noisy and not being able to sleep or get much work done, especially late at night and on weekends, some schools offer residences with "quiet floors." If this is truly a concern, then you may want to apply for housing on these floors. In general, almost all schools have policies regarding noise levels and usually set times (i.e. 10 p.m.) when loud music is no longer permitted. Like most things, life in residence will take some getting used to, and while at first it may seem noisy, you will quickly learn how to adapt in order to finish those term papers while still getting a good night's sleep.

The on-campus experience is indeed unique. Whether this uniqueness is good or bad, every student comes out of it with a different perspective on life and people in general. Residence, often viewed as synonymous to crazy events, late-night snacks, music all night long, and social games, has evolved throughout the years (although traces of such events still exist). While these sorts of day-to-day activities depend on what college or campus one attends, there is now a wide array of choices from the quiet residence to the more party-going life. Many students consider the experience a once-in-a-lifetime endeavour, while most leave the campus life for a more personal and quiet atmosphere where living is confined to a smaller amount of people. Nonetheless, before one takes this leap, consider the benefits and the costs of living on campus as well as the options one has in choosing the right place.

Choosing a Residence

- First, visit the campus to get a general sense of what college life is like. Try to sleep at a friend's place or simply visit a residence you are interested in and ask around. Get a more personal feel for the place, better than what a simple pamphlet may offer you. Seeing and partially living it is worth the expense and time because when it comes down to it, you will be living there for a whole year, so choosing well is essential. Living in an atmosphere that's not right for you is a way of possibly beginning your college experience on the wrong note. We strongly recommend that during your tour of the school at the open house, ask for a tour of the residences and possibly stay a night to get a real sense of the facilities.

• Read all the pamphlets and information you may receive through the mail; don't just choose randomly. Each residence has a particular feel, past history, and ambience and it's up to you to discover these and determine whether you are compatible. Figure out which residences are more prone to partying versus studying by asking previous students, friends who've attended the school, or house representatives who manage the residences. Choosing the wrong place is a cost in itself.

• Figure out the costs of living alone versus those of living with a roommate. Fees add up quickly, so take a moment to determine how you can reduce them and whether it's worth it. The general amount you will pay depends on the university and the residence. Newer residences with private bathrooms and single bedrooms will cost more but will add comfort. Older residences may offer a more authentic college experience, but is authentic what you are looking for? Rooms will vary everywhere whether you live alone or with a roommate. Meal plans will cost in addition to accommodation fees, council fees, and additional fees such as telephone, laundry, parking, and any other services.

Pros of Living On Campus

• Although residence life is more expensive in certain aspects, one must consider that many other costs are included in the actual price such as high-speed Internet, heating, electricity, water, satellite television, as well as the proximity to friends, the campus and its amenities, and laundry facilities.

• Although the meal plan may have certain flaws (weekends are often not covered and you may pay even though you do not eat certain meals), consider the benefits of having each meal cooked and prepared for you. Indeed, this detail makes campus food cheaper, and it's far more practical than having to go to the grocer and prepare a meal every time, especially when in a hurry.

• When it comes to transportation, closeness to campus is a definite benefit because you save time and money. You can walk to campus rather than take a bus or subway, which really comes in handy on those cold Canadian winter days. Social activities will be more residence-oriented therefore saving you certain expenses relating to extra travel.

• Furniture is provided by the residence and usually includes a basic table, lamp, desk, and shelves as well as a fridge and a "common area," all making campus life more convenient.

Cons of Living On Campus

• The food selection of meal plans is limited and restrictive. Most students tend to enjoy eating on the weekends when they can choose what food they want. The special meals lose their charm after several months of having the same old recipe over and over again. Furthermore, vegans and vegetarians—or simply any gourmet—may regret the "choice" of food offered in any campus cafeteria. Nonetheless, improvements are being made, as many independent food chains on campus become part of the meal plans.

• One critical issue is the extra cash one tends to spend on other, less valuable things such as outings, clothing, or late-night food delivery. One must realize that spending less on food and other essential things tends to promote more leisurely expenses such as decorations for the room or clothing.

• Since certain campus facilities do not offer weekend meal plans, the necessity of walking and finding a grocery store becomes evident. Finding the cheapest meals without sacrificing quality is a constant struggle but one that cannot be put aside.

For on-campus residency, prices will vary from the lower $1,000 to the upper $3,000 range, all depending on the quality of the location and services, so look early to increase the chances of securing your first choice. Most colleges and universities require you to send an application to be admitted in residence so send yours early and clearly state your top choices. If costs remain an issue, look into student loans and scholarships.

Living Off Campus

After the first year of college or university, many students are faced with the decision to either move off campus or continue to live in residence. Choices must be made and the search must be done efficiently and effectively to reduce costs and improve the chances of getting an ideal place. What are these critical steps? What type of decision must be made and when? What should you look for and what prices are best? These questions and more will be solved in the following part to aid your quest for the perfect apartment from start to finish. This thorough explanation will allow each student to understand the ins and outs of finding a place to live. Obviously, prices and circumstances will always vary depending on the individual, school, and city, but in the general scheme of things, all expenses are quite similar. It therefore comes down to finding the ideal location, and in order to achieve this goal you need to start early. Getting caught up in last-minute issues will simply complicate things as you will have to rush through the process thus increasing your chances of choosing incorrectly or even missing out on the option of choosing. Finding the ideal place is a time-consuming process, one that will necessitate much thought and organization, so read carefully as we guide you through it.

First, decide whether you want to live alone or with friends, and if you decide upon the latter, how many friends you will want to live with. This initial decision will be the starting point for any apartment search as prices and size will all depend on it. Second, take time out of your schedule to search for an apartment. Keep in mind that you are competing with all your peers in finding the best places to live, so unless you want to have to always go to someone else's place to hangout, stay committed and aware of the intense competition. Plan your time accordingly so you avoid putting off your search until after exams have finished, as chances are, most of the reasonably priced places near campus will have already been taken by this time. Plan to set aside the last two months of your second semester to find a place for the following year.

Searching and finding the right place at the right price is an art in and of itself. It usually requires visits to at least eight to ten different apartments/houses before you find one that meets your needs and wants and is still available when you call back the next day. Rents vary significantly from within a city or town, depending on how close to campus you want to live and the size of the city. You can spend as low as $200 per month on rent in a smaller town and you might be lucky and live relatively close to campus. But if you are looking to go to school in Toronto or Vancouver and live close to campus, plan on paying at least four to five times that amount. On average, you will probably be spending between $2,500 and $4,800 per year on rent while at school. Of course, the further away from campus you are willing to live, and the further away from downtown in the case of a big city, the cheaper your monthly rent will become. However, you should also consider whether the inconvenience of living further from campus will pose a problem of getting to class or to exams on time and whether there is decent public transit to get you to and from school.

Where to Look

Student settings are easy to find, either near the campus or relatively close to busy areas, but it is up to each student to disseminate from this vast array of information what exactly is worthwhile and what is not. You can easily narrow down your search by making a list of priorities or any other elements you deem as necessary or vital such as rent. By establishing a certain ideal location, you will be able to eliminate any bad choices without having to always linger over your decision. To gather information, students have many places to look, whether at the campus student-housing office, message boards across campus, college newspapers, university apartment complexes near and around campus, local papers, or even through other means such as friends, family, word of mouth, graduating students, and simply walking through any area you might be interested in—any means you use will allow you to gather more information. When initially beginning your search, there are multiple resources to consult: off-campus housing office, an online posting for students, or even billboards.

The off-campus housing office is usually run by the college or university and geared specifically to the needs of students. Most of the listings that are posted usually include the size of the apartment/house (i.e. how many bedrooms), the monthly rent, whether utilities are included in the rent, and how far it is from the campus.

If the housing office leads you to a dead end in the apartment search, try online postings through your school's web site or local newspaper housing ads, which can also often be found on the Internet. We offer a word of caution: the listings posted in the campus housing office or in newspapers are rarely verified to ensure that the information is correct. It's best if you write down all the information, especially the price, and bring it with you when you go to see the place to avoid any unfriendly surprises down the road if you are thinking about taking an apartment.

Your third option is to make a habit of reading the bulletin boards on campus because many students will use them to advertise an apartment or house that is or will soon be for rent. Furthermore, if you don't have any potential roommates in mind, this is a very good option since many students advertise for roommates to fill a vacant room in an apartment/house this way and can save you money by not having to buy furniture for a kitchen or living room.

Finally, remember that word of mouth is just as effective a method as all the rest, so keep your ears open. On many occasions, great housing that is cheap and close to campus is taken before it even goes on the market. Talk to your friends and others in your residence and get the word out that you are looking for a place by giving them specifics such as the size you are looking for and the price range you can afford. You never know, you might find a place through an unlikely source.

Make a List of Priorities

Now it's time to get things on paper and organize your thoughts and ideas on what you're looking for in an apartment. This is a very crucial step that you should never skip, considering that you'll most likely be spending thousands of dollars in rent over the next few years.

First, you should put together a range of what you're willing to spend on your apartment per month as well as a range for the total value. Afterwards, make a list of features and characteristics that you deem important to have in your apartment as well as a list of your most strong personality traits. Keep it simple and realistic and list them in order of priority since it can often prove difficult to find an accommodation that meets your exact criteria. Here is an example of what your lists may look like:

My Apartment Features:
• Separate entrance
• Washer/dryer included
• High-speed Internet hookup
• No basement apartments
• Lots of closet space
• Price: under $600 per month
• Utilities included

My Personality Traits:
• Independent
• Requires personal space
• Requires quiet time
• Penny-pincher

Analyze Your Lists

This next step involves putting a price tag on the items in your lists in order to determine which of the subsequent apartments you'll find during your physical search is the best buy for you. For example, in our sample list of apartment features, we would assign a value of $400 to item number two, a price found in a discount furniture-store flyer of a used washer/dryer set in acceptable condition. Note that this exercise will be hard to accomplish with some items, especially those in your personality-traits list, but try to approximate the values anyway. Remember that the ability to compromise is an invaluable skill when searching for an apartment; however, if there are items you simply cannot do without, indicate them on your list.

What to Look For

Based on your price and the number of people you will be living with, the range of possible places will automatically be reduced. But aside from these basic criteria, you have to consider many other things that may initially be deemed trivial (location, location, location: the well-known real-estate mantra bears much truth). Many factors come into play as you choose the ideal location; being near your campus is a definite plus as living in the "college ghetto" has a certain charm that simply cannot be replaced. Living near campus will save you time but keep in mind that such a benefit will lead to higher prices, so think twice about the importance of proximity. In fact, by not being entirely tied to the campus scenery you might be able to discover more than you expected from the city you live in; remember, your campus is only part of a city or town. Another issue often overlooked is the safety of the area. The typical student lifestyle often involves coming home late and, at times, alone. So please keep in mind that you are more susceptible in certain areas than others.

After finding the proper location, determine whether an apartment building or house is what you desire. Indeed, it all comes down to your own perception of what you will want and need in the future so keep that in mind at all times. Each type of place has its advantages and disadvantages and it will be up to you to determine which has more importance or value to you. Whether you prefer to have a doorman or live independently, live in an older charming house or an apartment, have a list of services offered to you or fend for yourself are all decisions you must make for yourself or with future roommates. And, of course, go into each visit with a critical eye. Check out the surroundings (locations of the grocery store, gym, campus, public transportation, bars, and/or park, etc.), the state of the property (cleanliness, security, age of building, and level of maintenance), and determine what sorts of people live around you. All these issues will undoubtedly affect your living experience and will therefore require some thought.

Once you've found listings that seem to fit your needs and budget, make sure to take note not only of the address and landlord's phone number but also of the price and other pertinent information. Students often show up at apartments to find that it's not the same thing as was listed or that the price has increased. If there are inconsistencies, demand the advertised price. (See the appendices for an apartment search checklist.)

What to look for in the perfect student living space:
• Do the appliances work? Check that the freezer and the oven work well.
• Can you drink the tap water? How is the supply of hot water?
• Check the condition of the shower, sink, and any other porcelain fixtures (leaking, cracks, mould, etc.).
• Is the apartment furnished? Is the furniture in good condition?
• Are the utilities included in the rent or will you be paying individual bills each month? Remember that paying for utilities is an important cost that can add up significantly (especially in winter months), so it's really important to consider these costs especially if the apartment is big and not well insulated.
• Is there enough light in the apartment and are there windows in many of the rooms?
• If there are windows at street level, can they be locked?

• How is the overall safety of the apartment? Is there a functioning smoke detector in the apartment? Check to see that there are proper emergency exits.

• Is extra storage space available?

• It is a good idea to find out from other tenants how quickly the landlord reacts to problems.

• What are the rules for living in the building (smoking, pets, noise, etc.)?

• Does the landlord live in the apartment building or nearby?

• Are there laundry facilities in the building? Where is the nearest laundromat?

• Walk around the neighbourhood to see how far away the closest grocery store is.

• How far is the closest bus stop?

• Find out from the landlord if he or she is planning on making any repairs to the apartment before you move in.

• Are there other students living in the building? We recommend knowing who your neighbours are. When you're with other students, you will have fewer problems because you will live a similar lifestyle and keep similar hours.

Reviewing the Lease Agreement

So you've found the ideal place and made up your mind. It's now time to take the final step and conclude the deal by signing the lease, which will enumerate all the rules and regulations you must obey for the length of your stay. All leases specify the general information such as the price, term length, costs, and regulations. Always be sure to read the document entirely before signing and confirming the binding agreement. Many details must be reviewed and identified as you read through the document, for they may affect you later on. Make sure the figures are stated and are the same as those mentioned by the landlord. Verify that all of the landlord duties are clearly stated in the text, and before moving in, run through any damage or maintenance that must be attended to. In terms of payment for the rent, many landlords require first and last month's in advance. In such situations, remember you are entitled to the interest on the last month's rent amount for the specified length of time so be sure that you receive the additional funds in the end. In case of any issues or arguments with your landlord, always keep a record of events and present them to an advisory centre at your school that will provide you guidance to solve your issue. When you are about to end your lease, remember to write a note prior to leaving as they are required by law, so take the time to write to your landlord to avoid the risk of having to pay for extra months.

Signing a lease is the most important step of the entire apartment search process, especially if it's the first time, as there are many things a student needs to go through before they sign. A lease is a legally binding contract—when you commit yourself, you can't go back on it and you need to agree with everything that is written in it. This is why it's really important to fully read the lease. Even if it is long, it is worth it. Remember to do a thorough apartment search before you sign a lease because once a lease is signed, you are committed to that living space.

You should go through these points before you sign:
• Make sure it is clearly written how much you will pay per month and what is included in that price (what the landlord pays for and what you will pay for).
• Verify if a security deposit is required, and if it is, find out what you need to do to be able to get it back at the end of the lease.
• Be sure the length of the lease is clearly stated. Generally, a lease will last for twelve months.
• If you have house pets, be sure there is not any pets clause within the lease, and if you are allergic to pets, be sure there is a no-pets clause written into the lease.
• Remember that every person who will be living in the apartment should sign the lease because it is only the lease signees that are committed and bound to the lease agreement.
• If the landlord committed to doing repairs on the apartment, then ask the landlord to document those repairs in writing so that you have them on record and can prove their commitment to you and your roommates.

• Read the rules of the apartment carefully, and fully agree to live by them.

• When you are getting ready to move out of your apartment, don't forget to give either thirty- or sixty-days notice before you leave because you are bound by law to inform the landlord of your intentions so that they have adequate time to advertise and find a new tenant.

Subletting

If you are going home for the summer and don't want to be stuck footing the bill for your rent while you're gone, subletting your apartment is the answer. If the housing market is tight and the vacancy rate low, you may even be able to charge more than is required to cover your monthly rent, making a little extra cash. The key to subletting is to advertise early. You will not be the only one trying to sublet a living space for the summer, so the earlier you get the word out that your place is available, the better chance you will have of finding someone.

Advertise anywhere and everywhere. You may want to start by placing an ad with the campus housing office, as there are often visiting students from other schools and abroad that come to study for the summer and one of the first places they will look for accommodation will be the housing office. Also, you will want to advertise on campus bulletin boards in addition to spreading the word amongst all your friends to see if they may know of anyone looking for a place during the summer. Finally, if you are not one for risks, you may want to look into paying for an ad in the local newspaper(s) to expand your search for that right summer tenant to the entire city or town. Also, if you live in a bustling city (i.e. Toronto, Vancouver, or Montreal) advertise through larger networks for tourists.

When deciding what the monthly rent should be for the sublet, consider all the wonderful features of your apartment. Remember that you are competing with other persons subletting, so market your place well and be sure to include every possible benefit your place has to offer. You should consider aspects such as:

- distance from campus;
- availability of air-conditioning;
- whether the building is quiet;
- laundry facilities in the building;
- the neighbourhood; and
- proximity of amenities (grocery store, pharmacy, etc.).

The number of aspects, as mentioned above, that your apartment includes can and should be reflected in a higher asking price. Conversely, the opposite is true as well. Asking a high price for an apartment that is far from campus, in a sketchy neighbourhood, and is far from most amenities probably won't get you too many takers.

Furthermore, you may also want to set two prices for your apartment, one if it is furnished and a second if it is unfurnished. This could save your furniture from being abused by a renter, even if it means having to move your furniture into storage. While storage fees are an extra cost, they most likely will be well below the money you will receive in rent each month, so you'll still be paying less than if the apartment sat vacant all summer. Also, if you pay utilities, it's advisable to have the tenant cover them for the summer because you don't want to be stuck paying for someone who leaves the lights on all the time and takes thirty-minute showers every day.

Once you have found someone to sublet your place for the summer or a portion of it, arrange to have the person sign an agreement. This agreement should explicitly state the monthly rent and any other obligations that they are responsible for, including payment for utilities and the phone bill in addition to compensation for any damages to the apartment or your furniture. We recommend you get a security deposit to cover any unforeseen issues that may arise at the end of the sublet. It's a good idea to approach the campus housing office for help with regards to drawing up a sublet agreement that covers all the relevant aspects. Upon the signing of the agreement, it is perfectly reasonable to ask for the first month's rent a few days in advance. Asking for postdated cheques for each month is reasonable as well because this will save you the hassle of having to chase after the person each month. To potentially avoid late payments to the phone company and a subsequent downgrading of your credit rating, its best if you transfer the phone line into the tenant's name just before you hand over the keys. Finally, arrange with the tenant ahead of time the means by which they will return the keys to you before they leave. This may seem obvious, but if the tenant accidentally walks off with the keys, this leaves you in a very difficult position.

To Buy or Not?

Another residency option is buying an apartment, condominium, or house. This is not feasible for all, but is possible for a few of you. Your parents can use the rent they collect from your roommates to help pay the mortgage, and there are many tax advantages that may be available to them if they choose to purchase a space. You or your parents should contact the Canada Revenue Agency (CRA) for further information regarding tax benefits. Purchasing property may be especially attractive if the housing market is still reasonably priced but is expected to appreciate in the next few years, providing your parents with a nice return on their investment. Also, it would ensure you a suitable place to live, especially if your chosen city or town has a low rental-vacancy rate, while not having to deal with the hassles of rent increases and lazy and/or uncooperative landlords.

However, there is always the possibility that with the unpredictability of the real-estate market, property values could depreciate. This would make your parents' investment in your education even more costly than they had anticipated, so be careful before rushing to make a decision in this matter. We advise you to get in contact with an established real-estate agent who knows the student market. In the end, if your parents decide to purchase property, they should definitely review the rules regarding rent controls and other bylaws pertaining to residential rental agreements before renting out rooms. In some cases, it may be difficult to obtain a mortgage if the property is being used as a rooming house. Shared accommodation with friends might be a better route to follow if your parents are buying a condo or house for your shared use.

By purchasing a location, you are guaranteed a place to live throughout your post-secondary years and even after your college experience. The value of the property may not only increase over the years, it will also allow you to rent out to friends and therefore provide you or your parents with a monthly income that will perhaps cover (we hope) most of your expenses. In terms of benefits for your parents, tax advantages are always a possibility, and the joy of not having to worry over rent or finding an apartment year after year is a great asset especially when many family members attend the same educational institution. Nonetheless, many disadvantages arise such as the risk of losing value over the years, issues over rent, tenant concerns, and all other worries and problems any lessee must go through on a daily basis.

Apartment Responsibilities and Considerations

So you've found the best place possible to live—the location is good, your neighbours seem nice, the people you live with are cool, everything seems to be going your way, so you decide to take a break, right? Wrong. As parents always tell their children, why put back what can be done today? Indeed, this motto, although a nuisance to hear for yet another time, is a truth that none can deny. An apartment is more than a roof, kitchen, bathroom, and a bunch of rooms; it requires care, decoration, and a sense of budgeting to make it more than just a place to live: a good place to live. Therefore, this section will cover some quantitative elements regarding utilities and other basic but necessary expenses. It will also take a qualitative view of apartment living by discussing furnishing and decorating.

Cost Considerations

- Utility costs: Although in this section we discuss costs after you've signed the lease, keep in mind that these are all issues that should be considered as you look at each potential accommodation. Indeed, looking at the apartment both as a whole and in detail while choosing your place to live will help you better determine total future costs and therefore save you time and avoid bad surprises.

In terms of utilities, always take a second look at things in front of you. Your apartment may be nice and big but what effect will this have for heating in winter? The kitchen is big and roomy, perfect for your extensive cooking habits, but there isn't a dishwasher—still in the mood to cook? Having no washer and dryer in the apartment may save you money for water bills but what if the closest machines are two blocks away? Although utilities are often considered as "extras," they nonetheless remain essential extras. Even with a relatively cheap rent per month, bills for heating, electricity, water, gas, Internet, cable, etc. may all add up and at times may equate to a sizable percentage of your actual rent. Consequently, we advise you to take a mental note of each and every issue you may need in the near future.

• Kitchen: Check for new utilities, cleanliness, gas or electricity, oven or microwave as well as the size of the fridge, freezer, and storage areas for all you heavy eaters or for those consciously choosing to stock up rather than having to purchase each and every week.

• Heating: For any individual living in Canada, this issue is of natural relevance and should therefore be taken very seriously. Always check the disposition of each place for its condition in terms of keeping heat inside the apartment rather than being drafty or unsealed. Is it isolated? Are the windows thin? Are there gaps near doors? Are the ceilings high? All these questions may seem time-consuming but are well worth the extra effort.

• Telephone: Local calls are never a major issue, but when it comes to long distance calling, shop around for the best plan and buy phone cards. We also highly recommend computer-savvy students to use free Internet services that allow you to talk online at no extra fee.

• Cable: Although your studies may consume most of your time, cable is always a nice way to wind down and relax. But for the little time you watch it, you must consider whether it is worth the cost. Living with friends can easily replace any television shows and always consider that a neighbour may watch the same shows as you.

• Parking: Depending on which city you live in, a car is either a hassle and burden or a godsend. But no matter where you go, the cost of parking remains the same. Unless you live in an apartment complex, having a parking spot may not be a given. To prepare yourself, you may need to wake up early and take the snow off the car each and every morning.

• Electricity: One simple concept to keep in mind here: if you pay for it, don't waste your money. Turn off the lights when you're not at home, don't have five appliances on at once, and if things get too dark at night in your room, try to share more light in the common room so more people can use the same light.

• Computer equipment and related elements: Most of the information here is generic but may be deemed as applicable. We recommend buying used since computers quickly become obsolete. But, most important, know what you need and don't need. Other considerations may include where one should purchase the equipment whether it is at a specialty store, an online store, a department store, or at warehouses. No matter how much information or tips one may give and provide to younger generations, the ultimate step is up to them when actually making the effort. Economics shows that the consumer can pay less by taking the time in finding the cheaper version, but out of convenience and time, we often don't. Therefore, there is a trade-off between the two.

Although it is impossible for us to predetermine all costs that may arise, we have covered the basics and suggest you simply keep an eye or conscious mind at all time on these extras.

Apartment Decoration

Now on to the more interesting part of having your own apartment: decoration. This one factor, of course, depends on personal style, flavour, interests, as well as on roommates and the actual layout of the place you have. In any case, in order to make the experience of living away from home a true second home, it is essential to make it personal and representative of yourself (while staying under budget, of course). First of all, get any furniture and gear you can get off your family members, not only because it's free but you also avoid a hassle of having to find basic things such as chairs, tables, and lamps (all things that remain relatively standard). Ask the previous tenant or owner of the apartment whether they would like to leave certain things behind. When it comes to less generic furniture, always start early and find things that are near your house. Living in a neighbourhood full of college students is ideal for furniture as all graduating students may have garage sales or may even simply leave extra stuff outside. It is therefore up to you to look around and try to get any information on what is happening in your area as soon as possible. As for posters and other more personalized accessories, try to find the cheapest deals first—you'll be amazed at how much interesting and cheap gadgets and decorations you may find at thrift stores, retro shops, or even small boutiques for far less than your typical brand-name logos.

A New Lifestyle

In terms of actual lifestyle, moving out of the home is a drastic change for most individuals. Having to do everything on your own is both one of the most desirable and overwhelming feelings in the world. Many students believe organizing and taking care of the house is a simple task (parents make it look simple) but when it comes to it, it truly is difficult and requires a lot of work, time, and effort. This section will simply run through useful guidance in keeping up with housework and school work while having an active social life.

- Wake up early: No matter how comfortable your bed may seem or how bad the weather may be outside, waking up early is perhaps the best decision you can make each day. With all your new-found activities, friends, and responsibilities, you will automatically require more time to balance everything fairly. Why waste half of your day accumulating more tasks for the following day when you could do everything that day?

• Cleanliness: Living in residence can be an eye-opening experience for many, but when it comes to your own house, pride is of the essence. To keep your house clean is more than a must, it is also a sign of order, maturity, and respect.

• Food shopping: Although buying quick and easy meals is ideal, especially when pressed for time, think of the money you are losing every time you spend over five dollars for a sandwich that can be made for a cost of two dollars or less. For all those who can't cook, begin the year with a resolution that will not only bring you pride but will save you money: take a cooking class. Although most are very basic they will guide you through the essentials of cooking and will therefore make going out to eat a pleasant option rather than a costly necessity. On a health-related note, keep in mind that purchasing microwavable and quick snacks is not a replacement for actual food. Furthermore, these meals cost more and your body requires more to feel satisfied. Saving money on food is often overlooked, but every dollar you save will inevitably add up. So choose a supermarket that caters to your budget and food selection, buy natural foods that cost less and are healthier, and take advantage of student discounts and coupons. All of these steps will allow you to not only have a greater variety of food but will also allow you to splurge from time to time.

• Social Engagements: When it comes to college and university, one of the first things that come to mind is student parties and events, which include drinking. Yet many students do not factor into their budgets the costs associated with drinking and attending social functions. Alcohol is an expensive commodity, one that many students pay for at the expense of other far more important aspects of life such as groceries or school supplies. If you do choose to have cocktails, a beer, or wine at night, we recommend you do so responsibly and in moderation. Being a responsible young adult means knowing your limits and the limits of those around you. Do not be afraid to suggest to people to stop drinking, and express concern if a person has clearly drank too much. When choosing to consume alcohol, there are ways of reducing the cost of doing so. A useful tip would be to drink with friends before going out at night; as a group, you can share the cost of the drinks and avoid the inflated costs at typical nightspots. We strongly recommend that you have glasses of water or juice between alcoholic beverages, as this practice will reduce the effect of the alcohol and keep you hydrated. And one final piece of advice: Never drink and drive nor get in a car with someone who has consumed more than an acceptable amount of alcohol. If you see a friend or someone who is about to drive while intoxicated, remove their keys and arrange for alternate transportation. By acting responsibly you may be saving someone's life.

When it comes to adapting to college, one must consider more than just the obvious changes. It will take most students their entire post-secondary experience to eventually be able to manage their budget effectively. But with this guide, you will gain a level of awareness that will enable you to manage and organize everything you need right off the bat. These first steps in managing your money, although only a beginning, will be a unique basis for your future life after school—a life where parents are no longer the suppliers of money.

As you can see, there are many elements related to living on one's own for the first time. Students must come to understand that this is not a one-time process but a continuous effort that will simply increase in routine as time goes by. We therefore ask you to be organized sooner than later as this is the best cost-saving advice out there. Take your time and think about all your options before you pick which one is best for you since your living arrangements can have a tremendous impact on how much you like college or university and how much you get out of the experience. Also, do not limit yourself simply to dollar figures because the most important advantages and disadvantages of each living arrangement may not be financial and it is impossible to put a dollar figure on things like learning to be independent or the safety of the familial home. Talk to your parents and see what they think about the issue since they most likely have valuable experiences to help guide you in your choices. Finally, start thinking about this early on, when you are selecting which school to attend, so you don't end up being forced into a living arrangement you don't care for.

Chapter Five
Making the Right Day-to-Day Choices

Having made choices on your accommodations, now it is time to apply yourself to make the right day-to-day choices to cut your monthly living expenses. Whether it is eating, having fun, purchasing household supplies, or using your utilities, the choices you make can impact your budget. But making the right choices is not always fun; it requires time, patience, and dedication. Making the right choices is the stepping stone to becoming a conscious consumer in a consumer-driven society.

After spending a lot of money on your tuition and rent, paying for the cost of going to university is not finished in the slightest. On top of these high costs for the tuition and rent, there are many additional expenses that students encounter while at school. Not only are these other expenses very high, they are also very difficult to budget appropriately. These other expenses will be broken down into additional costs of food, supplies, entertainment, travel, and extras. This chapter breaks down the extra expenses students face, and will enable you to better budget for them and come up with ways to save money.

Additional Living Costs Beyond Rent
Water & Electricity
It is not entirely obvious that to save money you need to become an environmentally aware consumer. In some instances, being environmentally unfriendly will become costly. A general

rule is less is more. Use less water. Use less electricity. If you do this, you will save money when you receive your electric and water bill. Energy-efficient appliances are sometimes more expensive than regular appliances and will make an immediate impact on your budget. In the long run, however, they will make a big difference in the amount you pay over time.

When people pay their rent, there is a tendency to believe that the majority of their expenses are taken care of. The reality, however, is that a lot of residences where students tend to live do not include the cost of utilities such as hydro and gas within the rental price. Hydro is a large expense, especially in the winter, and many cities do not have many companies to choose from. What you should look out for to create a reasonable budget is to pick a company that allows you to pay the same monthly payments throughout the year. If you don't do this, you will have extremely large bills in the winter and small bills in the summer. Depending on how cold it gets outside, the winter bill could be enormous. For this reason, we strongly recommend you thoroughly research the average winter and summer utility costs for the location you move into.

Telephone, Cable TV, & Internet Service

Beyond hydro, the other expenses for your apartment include telephone service, cable or satellite television, and Internet service. Depending on which company you are going with, there are many possible ways of bundling these services together and subsequently paying a lower monthly bill for the three together.

Most cities have a choice of one or two telephone providers, but this number is likely to expand in the future. Also, the Internet can be provided through a telephone line or cable line. For high speed, the cost of either type is quite similar, and the lower one will depend on if you are bundling another service with one company. The option of high-speed Internet also depends on the availability in the region. Even today, many places do not have access to high-speed Internet. Finally, the television gives you the option of cable or satellite. If you wanted to go with a lower cost, the basic television service is the way to go. Although you get fewer channels than with digital cable or satellite services, it is around half the cost. If you are a television junkie, then digital cable or satellite is the way to go. Both are very similar in terms of cost, quality, and variety of channels. The one to choose would again be the bundle that gives you the best deal. Also, you should watch out as some landlords do not allow satellites to be installed on their buildings, so make sure to ask beforehand.

If you are living on your own and studying full-time, you will probably not be watching television very often or not as often as you did before. Depending on the number of cable- or satellite-service suppliers in your area, prices can vary, but most of the time it is quite expensive for any kind of cable service. Find out what these suppliers offer including the number of channels, the types of channels, the quality of the signal, and the price. Satellite service is more complicated to install and maintain. Some land-lords do not allow satellite dishes to be in visible areas, while others ban satellite dishes altogether. Satellite service can become expensive depending on the packages you sign up for.

The Internet is also a good place to catch up on your television favourites. Various sites provide resumés of entire episodes in order to follow your favourite television personalities. So if you don't have access to television, you will still have the Internet. However, if you feel like you cannot survive without television, some basic cable service provides a great variety of American shows through local channels.

Another alternative to missing some of your favourite series is to wait for it to be released in your local movie-rental store. It is becoming more of a trend to pick up your favourite series at your local video store because an increasing number of them are being released on DVD right after the season has ended. Even your old favourites may find themselves on shelves near you.

These three extras, which are almost a necessity for some students, are quite expensive. Having high-speed Internet, a telephone line, and digital cable can cost upwards of $200 per month. If this is too high for you, then there are cheaper alternatives to consider. Instead of having Internet at home, almost every university has a computer lab for students to use free of charge, and many are open for twenty-four hours a day. Although it may be a little less convenient, it can save you hundreds of dollars per year. It is possible to make it through school without having cable, and you can just find a friend who has cable and go over to watch when a show you want to see is on. Finally, instead of having a traditional land-line telephone, many students today simply have a cellphone. We recommend you at least consider the cellphone alternative. Many students have both a land line and a cellphone, and, in many cases, the land line becomes just an additional expense. You can get a cellphone plan very cheap, so it might be worthwhile to forgo the land line and stick with just the cellphone.

Groceries

Food in general is one expense category that is guaranteed to become one of the largest expenses in your monthly budget. Whether it is buying groceries, dining out, or purchasing your daily coffee, the tiny amount spent here and there can and will add up quickly. The more you save on groceries, the more money you will have to spend elsewhere.

Food is a huge expense for the average student, no matter if you are in your first year living in university residence or living on your own in an independent living situation. Although there is a great temptation for students to shop for cheaper junk food, it is definitely worthwhile to make healthier choices concerning food. This does not mean you will pay a lot more, but it does mean you must become knowledgeable in food shopping before going to the store for the first time. If you don't, the trip will be inefficient and will end up costing you too much. Parents should encourage their children to venture out in the grocery store with them before going away to school to afford them the necessary experience and knowledge about the operations of a typical grocery store.

Selecting a Grocery Store

One of the big issues with food is selecting the store that best fulfills your needs. There are many selections out there so this will break down the different types of stores that you can choose from. One must remember that the biggest factor while selecting your grocery store is the proximity to your apartment. Although you might be able to save more money venturing out around the city, the amount of time spent transporting yourself and your food might negate any savings you get from buying less-expensive food.

There are many different types of stores to choose from, including chain grocery stores, co-op stores, warehouse clubs, markets, bulk-food stores, and convenience stores. There are advantages and disadvantages to each type of store based on the hours of operations, location, quality of food, selection, and relative prices. No matter which one you choose, however, there are certain things you must remember when going shopping. Once you've chosen your store, remember the following:

- Don't assume that everything at a warehouse club is a great deal simply because it comes in a big container. In some cases, it may be cheaper to buy certain items at a grocery or convenience store (i.e. milk, bread, eggs, etc.).
- At supermarket chains, consider purchasing the house-brand products instead of name-brand products. House brands are often substantially cheaper and are, in many cases, produced at the same plant as the name brands. Chances are that when you are dipping your nachos into the house-brand sour cream, you won't be able to tell it from the national name brand.
- When shopping in supermarkets (or any stores), if you find a discrepancy between the advertised price and the actual price, draw it to the clerk's attention and ask for an explanation. Through experience, we have found that the store will often greatly reduce the item or even give it to you to avoid any publicity of their "error."
- Impulse buying is a real problem, particularly in warehouse clubs. There are so many interesting items for sale (in addition to food) at very low prices that it becomes easy to get caught up in a buying frenzy. You may find yourself buying an electric cooler that you may only use once or twice a year! So, once again, stick to your list.
- Watch the register when your items are being rung through. By the end of the day, many cashier clerks may

miss the sale price on the cartload of broccoli that you're stocking up on or the bar code has not been updated to reflect the sale on the register.

Many manufacturers and retailers entice shoppers to buy in large quantities by offering substantial savings on jumbo-size items. However, what is a student supposed to do with a two-gallon drum of mustard or a 100-pack of hamburger buns? Not only do you require your own warehouse to store these purchases but you also require a bigger budget. In the case of perishable goods, we have found that they often go bad before you have a chance to use them, thereby negating any possible savings. In this environment of super-bargain-bonus-extra-value-saver packs, how can the single student get a good deal?

• Look for weekly specials on products in smaller sizes. These are often priced as "loss leaders" (items sold by retailers at or below cost) in order to lure customers into their store.
• Purchase in bulk-food sections whenever possible. This way you can buy the exact quantity you want at the same price as someone buying ten times that amount. Spices, flour, cereal, and nuts are just a few examples of products sold in bulk. Incidentally, you also save money on fancy packaging and help the environment.
• Go together with roommates to take advantage of bulk buying on frequently used items and necessities such as milk, toilet paper, hand soap, laundry and dish detergent, plastic wrap, light bulbs, and multipurpose cleaners. We have found it works well for an individual to make the purchase at the store and then for the itemized receipt to be split up between roommates (other roommates write a cheque to the purchaser for their percentage of the total bill).
• Stock up on the manufacturers' discount coupons that are frequently available in store aisles or on product packages, particularly if they are for items that you use a lot.

The advantage of these coupons over store-issued coupons is that they can be used at almost all stores and they often have no (or at least a distant) expiry date. If you buy a certain brand of cereal and there is a stack of coupons in the store, stock up—they may last you the entire year.

• Find out if your grocer offers a student discount. Some markets or grocers offer discounts to students and seniors on certain days of the week.

Grocery Shopping: The Basics

Without a doubt, eating in rather than dining out is cheaper—cheaper by a long shot. Groceries used for eating in, however, can become very expensive if they are not purchased wisely. First and foremost, the rule of thumb is to never buy groceries hungry or on an empty stomach. An empty stomach will influence the amount of food you buy at the store; if you are hungry, you are more likely to purchase food impulsively, meaning without a true reason or need for doing so. Your mood also sets you up to make impulsive food purchases because of how it affects your behaviour. Whether you are angry or tired, what you buy will reflect your mood. When people are tired, they try to get more energy through food and tend to make incorrect choices: more sweets and high-carbohydrate foods. When people are angry, they choose crunch food—the junk food. The time at which you decide to go grocery shopping is also a factor. Shopping in a quiet setting such as in the morning or late at night (after 8 p.m.) will allow you to be more time efficient in picking your items and allow you to leave more easily and quickly without the hassle of long lines. Another advantage of shopping during the quieter hours is that you will be able to make better, less distracted decisions in terms of your purchases.

When you go shopping on a full stomach and in with the correct mindset to buy groceries, you will avoid overspending and will make solid healthy food choices. Below is a list of diagnostic questions to ask yourself when you begin to do your own food shopping. They are meant to give you structure and make food shopping less overwhelming.

• Do you have a planned food budget?

- Do you have the time to shop?
- Do you take the time to survey the local grocery-store flyers on their specials?
- Do you clip coupons?
- Do you make a list of what items from the grocery store you will need?
- Do you check your refrigerator and pantry before making your list of groceries needed?
- Are your items on your list food products?
- Do you like to cook?
- Do you have the time to cook?
- Do you properly store your food?
- Do you always freeze your leftovers?

If you answered "yes" to all these questions, then you are on your way to saving money on your groceries. However, for those who answered some with "no," here are a few things you should know:

- Knowing how much money you have allocated for your groceries will prompt you to check grocery-store flyers for specials and motivate you to stay within your budget.
- Clipping coupons can save you plenty even though the amounts sometime seem minuscule. A few cents or dollars saved here and there can easily add up to a big amount saved at the end of the year.
- Listing what you believe you need and checking your food inventory will help you manage what you truly need when you go to the market. And with your list in hand, you will be less likely to buy items that are expensive and/or not on your list.
- You should never buy household commodities (unless they are on special) in a grocery store. Stick primarily to food items when you go to the supermarket and survey other retail stores for those household commodities.
- Typically, local seasonal fresh produce will be much cheaper if it is purchased in the right quantities. All spoilage of unused fresh produce becomes money dumped

in the garbage can. Prepared frozen food is slightly more expensive and the sizes available to your disposition typically benefit the larger sizes. Never underestimate the availability of canned goods for items that are not seasonal or are out of season.

• Generic brands are cheaper than brand names. Unless you have had a terrible experience with a generic brand, these items are perfect substitutes.

• Stores will display the higher-priced items at your chest level for convenience purchasing; therefore, you should scan the top and the bottom shelves to see if you can get a better deal on the same type of product.

• Storing your food properly will guarantee the freshness of your produce longer: freeze raw meat immediately after purchase and defrost what you need.

• Freezing your leftovers will help you avoid spoilage. Be sure to mark the date that it was made and what it is to ensure that you do not forget it in your freezer for too long.

An important thing you should not forget to do is to check your receipt before leaving the store. Price mistakes are likely to occur and it is usually to the grocery store's advantage. You can also create a book to record the items you've purchased and their original and special prices to keep track of the pricing. This will also save you time when it comes to deciding what food commodities to buy and where. Grocery shopping is an activity that requires time—the more time you put in it, the more money you will save in the long run.

Meal Expenses

Dining Out

Although buying groceries and cooking your meals is the wiser choice in terms of cost, you should not deprive yourself of the possibility of eating out. Monitor how frequently you eat out, where you are dining out, what you ordered, and how much it costs. There are ways to save when eating out. It all starts where you choose to eat. Some restaurants are pricier in certain areas than others, while others offer great-quality food for a more reasonable price. Outside of restaurant choice, there are other things you can do to cut your bill down:

• Know the restaurant policy in terms of sharing a plate with somebody, not ordering anything, tipping, and the cost of modifying what you ordered before you enter the restaurant.
• You should stick to your glass of water. Alcohol and beverages tend to be overpriced in restaurants and vary in sizes. If you are keen on drinking something, you should probably consider dining in a bring-your-own-wine restaurant. Alcohol is a big cash cow for restaurants: the mark-up is huge, taxes are high, and you tip on top of it all. When dining out, set a limit ahead of time on how much you'll consume. It is easy to spend two or three times more on beverages than on food. If you're going to drink, a better option is to have a drink at home before you go—a much cheaper alternative! When ordering wine, pass on the cork sniffing and order the house wine. Most restaurants use a popular brand with wide appeal and a much lower price. (If you drink, we recommend that you do so in moderation and responsibly.)
• Evaluate the daily specials or the table d'hôte. Restaurants typically offer three-course meals with table d'hôte for a fraction of the price.
• If you are not very hungry, you should consider either ordering from the appetizers section or sharing a meal with somebody. But beware of the possible extra charges that may be added because you are sharing, and some restaurants do not even allow you to share your meal. Another good choice is considering plates that offer you two sizes: junior size or full size. But if your are really keen on ordering what you had your stomach set on, you could always doggy bag the rest and make a meal out of it the following day.
• If you doggy bag anything, do not ask them to use another type of container instead of the standard one. Some restaurants charge extra for the use of a different container.

It is obvious that you are not always going to want to eat at home. Sometimes that three-day-old meatloaf in the fridge just isn't going to make you salivate. When you do eat out, follow these strategies to ensure you get maximum food value for your money:

• Use coupons when you can. Restaurants want students' business and they will usually offer coupons to get you there. Student newspapers and coupon mail-outs are the best place to find them. The best times to find coupons in student newspapers include the beginning of school (orientation-week kits are also often full of money-saving coupons), homecoming weekend, and after reading week (they know you're broke by then).

• Take advantage of the all-you-can-eat buffet or student specials.

• Take advantage of special "student nights." Many restaurants offer a particular night, such as "2-for-1 Tuesdays," when the eats are cheap. If you play it right, you can literally find a student special somewhere every night of the week.

• Especially when ordering spicy food, cut down your drink costs by ordering a pitcher of water from the start. Many restaurants love to add a little zing to their dishes to spice up the old bar sales.

• Some eating places are divided into a restaurant section and a pub section. The food in the pub is often very similar in taste but much cheaper. Eat there and save.

• Take advantage of off-hour specials that many restaurants offer for those who dine at non-peak hours. Big discounts are sometimes given to those who eat before 5 p.m. This is an inconvenient time for some people but is often perfect for students, who, perhaps, have to catch a night class anyway.

• If you are looking for good nutritious food at student prices, consider delis or market eateries where you don't have to pay for service and thus avoid the tipping costs.

• Larger companies and their marketing agencies have recently discovered that the college and university market is huge—as much as $4 to $5 billion in discretionary income. (How did they ever miss it?) In response, advertisers have decided this is a population definitely worth targeting. Their student marketing campaigns now include travelling carnivals where free samples and coupons are offered for everything from breakfast pastries to macaroni and cheese (as well as non-food items such as deodorants, shampoos, and perfumes). So grab your knapsack, laundry bag, backpack, and suitcase and generously help yourself to these travelling "freebie fiestas."

• Hospital cafeterias are often cheaper than the campus cafeteria. I know that's probably not the place you want to go on a first date, but you can buy a reasonably priced meal for those times when it's just your stomach that needs to be satisfied. A fair number of universities or colleges have hospitals either on campus or nearby, which makes the hospital cafeteria a convenient place to grab a cheap lunch or dinner.

• Specialty coffee shops have become the trend in recent years with each one trying to outdo the others by selling a more exotic gourmet blend. Needless to say, their popularity comes at a cost. If you have become one of the converted caffeine connoisseurs, then consider buying a coffee maker and some good beans to brew at home.

• If it is the coffee-shop atmosphere you enjoy and there is one particular café you like, then ask if they have a frequent-drinker card. Many retailers want your loyalty and offer a free cup for, say, every sixth cup you buy as an incentive to return. Not a huge bonus but nevertheless a roughly 20% savings to you.

Obviously, you will not adopt all of these suggestions for saving money on food, but if you adopt the ones that fit your timetable and lifestyle, then you should save a bundle. Eat, enjoy, and keep your stomach and wallet full!

Ordering Takeout Food

Although you are trying to cut your restaurant bill, one thing you should remember is to tip your waiter or waitress no matter how much your bill has amounted to. If you really want to avoid tipping, you should consider getting takeout, where tipping is not expected but usually appreciated. A few things to look for when you opt for dining at home with takeout food:

- Pick up your order. You should never get it delivered because most restaurants have a minimum amount required for free delivery or their amount differs from that of the takeout counter by a dollar or so.
- Know about specials available when you order directly from the takeout counter than by phone.
- If you have coupons that are good for takeout, use them. Newspaper and weekly flyers are a good place to look for coupons. You could also purchase a coupon book dedicated to eating out which can save you plenty of money.
- Make sure they do not charge for special containers that you did not request.

Dining at a restaurant or eating takeout can become costly. With the proper research beforehand, you will be able to save and avoid any type of additional costs that may be incurred. Nevertheless, it is the more expensive option between cooking the meal yourself and ordering the meal. But as long as it is done in moderation, you can peacefully and economically enjoy your meal.

Lunchtime Meals & Campus Food Plans

Lunch

Perhaps the most regular and costly drain on a student's funds is lunch. In the haste to make that 8 a.m. class, students will often forgo breakfast only to find themselves famished by lunchtime and shelling out $7 to $10 for a prepared lunch on campus. Not only is campus food likely to leave a nutritional void but it's also more expensive since you are paying for overhead and preparation costs, and the meal may be taxed as well. Eating on campus can mean an extra cost of $4 to $5 per day ($80 to $100 per month) on lunches alone! An easy solution is preparing lunches that are far more nutritional in value at a fraction of the cost. Most food you buy and prepare yourself is tax-free and the overhead is low. We offer some suggestions:

• Buy fruit such as oranges, apples, and plums that can be easily carried around in your knapsack without being squashed (avoid pears, overripe bananas, peaches, etc.). If you really crave these softer fruits, cut them up ahead of time and carry them in a resealable container to keep them fresh and leak-proof.

• Premixed salad in a resealable plastic container (with the dressing in a separate container) should remain fresh for nearly a day—a much cheaper route than buying.

• Purchase large bags of chips, nuts, cookies, gummy bears, squares, bagels, etc. and divide them up into resealable bags. This is much cheaper than buying individual bags of these same items. Make them up at the beginning of the week and they'll be ready to take in your knapsack each day.

• Many campus cafeterias have microwaves available for use at no charge. Take meat or cheese sandwiches, leftover pizza, chili, lasagna, etc. to heat for lunch. This gives you some variety and will help avoid that dreaded "lunch-bag letdown."

Campus Meal Plans:
• Try to get a meal plan that fits your eating habits.
• Most meal plans operate on a point-of-cash debit system. Make sure that if you buy a plan such as this you can be refunded for points not used at the end of the school year.
• Some meal plans may allow you to purchase alcohol at on-campus licensed establishments. Avoid ever using this option! You may run out of meal-plan points by January if you abuse it.

• If you tend to devour anything in sight and your eating has caused the occasional food shortage, the cheapest option for you may be to purchase an all-you-can-eat meal plan, which some schools offer.

Additional Tips for Off-Campus Students

Many campuses offer cafeteria meal plans for off-campus students. If you spend a lot of time on campus, have only a short break for dinner, or live far from campus, it may be worth your while to purchase a meal plan for one meal a day. It is probably cheaper and more time-efficient than trying to make it home to eat. If you are not inclined to use the stove at home, then it might also be one way to ensure you have one hot meal per day.

Purchasing Textbooks

Many universities give their students estimates on how much their supplies will cost per year. These figures, however, are almost always dramatically underestimated. For some reason, the textbook publishing companies believe in charging an exorbitant amount of money for books and this expense adds up very quickly each semester. Since there is usually a correlation between a book purchased for a course and the mark or grade received in the class, we will discuss ways in which you can purchase your class book without paying too much for it. With the average cost of textbooks coming to about $100 a piece, one of the best options to consider is finding used versions of your textbooks. Many bookstores on campuses sell limited supplies of used texts, so we recommend you beat the rush and attempt to buy your texts as early as possible. On this note, if your university's bookstore does not sell used texts or is currently out of the used version of the text you need, shop the local second-hand bookstores which typically abound in university neighbourhoods.

Students who took the course previously are also looking to get rid of their old textbooks. Keep an eye open for posters around your campus and keep your ears open for friends who have taken the class. Even if a newer version of the book has come out, the differences are usually minimal and any supplemental readings can be found easily.

Our advice to you is to first make sure the textbook is required for the class. Sometimes the professor may list it as a resource but not a necessary reading. If this is the case, purchasing the book is not really necessary and there will most likely be a copy of any non-required texts on reserve at your campus library or your specific faculty's library. If the book is required, buy the book by yourself and look for a used copy first. Get to the bookstore early to increase the likelihood of finding a used copy, and if they are sold out, stop by the local used bookstore to try your luck. Remember, paying $40 instead of $100 for a text makes the search worth a few hours of your time. Also, when you do buy the book, make sure you keep it in good shape to get the best possible resale value afterwards.

Most students have barely gotten over their tuition bills when they get sideswiped by book lists. Students can easily drop from $600 to $1,100 on a year's worth of books. While you can't eliminate this expense, you can cut it down. The first step is to categorize the books on your list. Start by determining which books are absolutely essential to the course and which ones are additional or optional. Then, figure out which are the most important secondary books and which ones are suggested reading only. Once you've categorized the list, you can make smarter choices about where to spend money and where to cut corners.

Main Textbooks

These are the ones you are absolutely going to need, so it's not worth forgoing them to save cash. You'll probably want to review the readings when exams arrive, so it's better to own these books rather than hoping to find them in the library when everyone else wants them too. Many students make notes in their textbooks, which are also convenient at exam time.

Secondary Textbooks

These are quite important and you will need them, but you may be able to get these secondary books by borrowing them from the library or by getting together with a friend in the same course and splitting the cost. If you know someone who took the course before, you can perhaps borrow his or her books. If you make good notes from these, you may not even need to have a copy of the books around when exam time comes.

Suggested Readings

In many courses, the main readings are so heavy that you'll never make it to suggested readings, so don't run out and buy all these right away. This is the best place to scrimp by borrowing from the library or even from your professor. (Some people never make it past the main textbook, so your professor will think you are really keen if you're doing the suggested readings!) With some textbooks, the only way you'll end up reading them is if you are snowed in with a broken TV on a Friday night.

How to Buy Textbooks: Literal Savings

Get your reading list early so that you can get your books ahead of the stampede at the start of term. Many professors have their book lists available prior to the start of school, usually in printed form but sometimes online.

Before you head straight to the campus bookstore to buy a brand new copy, try instead to pick up your main texts and any supplementary reading you want from the following sources:

- Trade online: You can now buy, sell, or exchange textbooks without forking over the commissions that many used bookstores charge—meaning more money in your pocket. A completely free service is www.textbook trader.ca
- Check used bookstores: Many colleges and universities operate these on campus as a service to students, and most towns have at least one near the school. You'll pay much less than at a new bookstore.
- Talk to friends who took the course to see if they'll lend or sell you their books. They'll probably give you a good deal.
- Check "For Sale" boards, department bulletin boards, and student newspapers for used texts for sale. In addition, put up a posting advertising the books you'd like to buy.

• Talk to your professors: They sometimes have a few spare copies and will lend you one for the year (or sell to you at a discount). If they wrote the book, they'll probably have plenty of autographed copies sitting on their office shelves collecting dust.

Here are some things to watch for when buying used (or even new) books:

• Check against the reading list carefully to see that you have the correct edition. You don't want to get stuck with an old edition when the professor is using a revised version.

• If you get stuck with an old version, don't run out to buy the revised edition before you check with your professor to see if it matters—the changes could be minor.

• Try to get used textbooks from someone who did well in the course. That way, any highlights or notes in the margin will be more valuable than if you get the text from someone who only got a D-. On the other hand, a student who received a D- in the course may have never "cracked the spine" of the book, and you could find yourself buying a brand-new never-read copy of the text at a reduced price!

Computer Expense

Other than books, the other major expenditure is on a computer. With the advances in technology, desktop computers can be purchased for less than $400. The convenience of having your own computer is worth the cost even with most schools giving access to students to computers at all hours of the day. When you need to use a computer the most, it seems everyone else wants to use one as well, making it extremely difficult to get your work done. This is the reason why we strongly suggest you invest in your own personal computer.

When you make the choice to invest in a computer, there are many options out there for the student. There are many places that sell used computers, but we recommend a new one as this comes with a better warranty in most cases. As computers continue to grow in popularity, more and more stores and retailers are cropping up to grab a piece of the action. Not only do you have a confusing selection of brands but also different ways you can buy. The following gives a list of places to purchase a computer and the pros and cons of each place:

• Specialty stores: The specialty computer store emphasizes knowledgeable staff, personal service, and technical support. However, you'll sometimes pay a significantly higher price (up to 15% to 25% more) than that of discount stores.

• Custom builders: These are tech whizzes turned entrepreneurs who assemble computers to your liking ... sort of like designer computers. Sound expensive? Well, not necessarily. Some of these people are hobbyists; they often work out of their own home or apartment, meaning low overhead, some great prices, and you can get some personalized service. The only drawback is that because it's a hobby or part-time business, they may not have the business two or three years from now.

• Office superstores: They often have excellent prices and good warranties. The only problem is you usually don't get the support of knowledgeable staff—a real drawback if you're just entering the computer age.

• Computer superstores: These stores give great prices and have excellent selection, although the staff can tend to lack knowledge. Ask a department manager to serve you in this situation since they probably have better knowledge or bring a computer-whiz friend to the store with you.

• Warehouse clubs: These places thrive on low prices. Selection, however, is limited, which makes comparison-shopping difficult. You'll probably get the least knowledgeable staff here, so short of pointing out the power switch, don't expect much from them. For some purchases, these stores are great, but for a computer, you may want to focus on the other retail options.

• Direct order and online retailers: Although direct order houses don't give you that hands-on feeling, they can give you some great prices. These places are particularly good when you already know what you want to buy. If you consider these options, keep the following points in mind:

  • Make sure they have twenty-four-hour service to assist you with technical problems (usually a toll-free number).

  • Find out if they will send a service person to your house if something breaks down or if you have to ship the computer back to the manufacturer. Shipping can be expensive and time-consuming. If there is a major technical problem, will they send a free replacement machine while they fix yours? Your professors may not buy the "technical difficulties" line as an excuse for a missed deadline.

  • Pay by credit card rather than cheque. If there's a problem, you can stop payment through a "charge back" by the card company.

  • Order only from established reputable companies. There are plenty of fly-by-night companies that may disappear long before the warranty expires.

  • If you are ordering from a U.S. company, check on delivery time in Canada. Delays at customs are common. Also, check on who pays the shipping charges and the validity of the warranty in Canada.

We recommend that you invest in a warranty for the computer if one is not already included. You don't want to be faced with the expenses to replace the hard drive, getting a new operating system, getting a new battery, and spending hours on tech support figuring out how to get it working. Also, you should consider what the computer will be used for and then buy one powerful enough to meet your needs. If all you will be doing is word processing and surfing the web, the top-of-the-line computer is not going to benefit you enough to justify the cost. Learn more about your program of study and see what sort of computer software you will be using. Other suggestions for purchasing a computer include:

• Shop around and compare carefully. Some retailers will beat a competitor's price by as much as 10% of the difference if you tell them or show them the competitor's price (such as in a flyer). If service and support are your top concerns but you see a much better price at a superstore, see if the store with the service you want will meet the superstore price. Some will, just to get your business.

• Many systems have very subtle but important differences. Write down particulars to help you compare.

• Try to keep your options open. Some computers can be upgraded without spending a fortune to do it. This could mean big savings in the future.

• When buying any computer equipment or accessories, ask what the price is rather than assuming it is still the advertised price. The industry is releasing newer models so rapidly that the price on the slightly older model you've chosen may be cheaper than the price marked or advertised the previous day.

Other Supplies

The final types of supplies you will need are pens, paper, notebooks, calculators, etc. These supplies can be found very cheap at back-to-school sales, and once you get some binders, they can be reused each semester. Be careful of the prices at the university bookstore or supply store at your school; although these retailers are convenient, their prices will be higher, reflecting their unique location near students. If possible, try to drive out of the university setting and go to a big retailer, possibly the same one at which you purchased your high-school supplies as their prices will be lower and you will not deal with the very long lineups that frequently form at university bookstores at the beginning of each semester. Overall, the costs of these supplies are definitely not a major cost consideration to worry about.

The Cellphone Era

Nowadays, the cellular service companies are continually trying to outdo each other's promotions. How can you benefit from this fierce competition? How do you make the right decision in terms of your needs? First, you must determine what your needs are. What is your usage pattern? Are you a frequent and constant user or are you a mild user? Are you shopping for a new phone or are you only shopping for a calling plan?

If you are a frequent user, make sure you have the right plan. The wrong calling plan can hurt your budget. Frequent users will usually sign short- or long-term contracts with the cellular service companies and will, in return, receive a new phone for free. However, watch out for additional charges such as activation, access, directory, and assistance fees. You should also consider asking your close friends which company and which phone they use, to get a better assessment of the service, charges, and phones; there is nothing more honest than your friend's evaluation of a product or service they use. Also, living in the competitive market of cellular service, make sure you read all the fine print involved when you sign the contract. Make sure you know what services you are getting for free and for how long and what kind of service you are generally paying for. For example:

- roaming charges?
- long-distance rate?
- cancelling charge?
- what time is considered the beginning of evening rates?
- when does the period end for weekend calling?

Due to the fierce competition between service providers, one company will typically offer to buy your contract and give you a better deal and a better phone. You can take advantage of this by simply getting one company to buy out another until a better offer comes along. Or if you simply want a new cellphone and you are content with your service, you could renew your current contract and you may be given a new phone.

If you are not a frequent user, you should go with a prepaid card plan. You have access to all the features albeit limited usage and you control how much time you want to purchase. At the expiration of your prepaid card, if you have any unused minutes, you can collect those minutes by simply buying another prepaid card. Some people will only buy ten minutes every month, while others may have fluctuating usage—you control how much you want to spend. The disadvantage of being a prepaid-plan user is that you pay all the fees and you have to pay for your cellphone.

No matter what your habits are, you should never be making long-distance phone calls from your cellphone unless it is an emergency. Roaming charges and long-distance charges can easily accumulate into a large unnecessary sum on your monthly bill or deducted from your prepaid phone card. These amounts can be avoided by simply choosing the smarter choice of calling either from a pay phone or from home or other land line if necessary. Screening your phone calls is also wise. If you have voice-mail access on your cellphone, definitely let the voice mail pick up phone calls from telephone numbers you do not recognize and check your voice mail through a land line because most companies will not charge you if you check it this way. Wasting your airtime minutes on a wrong number can become costly if it happens too frequently.

Long-Distance Calling

For students who live away from their homes, family, and friends, they may call home once in a while or, perhaps, more frequently. Long-distance charges from your land-line telephone supplier may not totally be to your advantage. Land-line suppliers' deals are usually very complicated. However, using the Internet to research the best options can easily facilitate making the right choices. Calling cards are also another alternative. But the cheapest way to communicate is using the Internet to communicate with one another via web-cam and audio conversations.

With a land-line supplier, calling long distance can become costly if you do not know your rates for different areas or countries. On an international basis, calling outside the continent can be very expensive, so research the right plan that suits the usage pattern of your long-distance calling—where will you be calling?

How long do you intend or typically talk to this person? How frequently will you be calling? Some companies offer bundle packages such as a flat fee for anywhere calls within Canada or special rates for same-province calling. Whichever company you decide to use, make sure before signing or agreeing to a contract to know all the services and fees that you will be expected to pay.

Some prefer using calling cards from different independent long-distance service providers especially for international calls. However, there are so many calling cards on the market that you should make sure which cards are better suited for your long-distance calling habits as well as any type of fees they may charge such as activation fees and connection fees. Calling cards are available on a global basis; therefore, if you purchased a card in Europe or Asia, it may not be valid in the Americas, and so you should make sure the 1-800 number is a valid number in your region to avoid paying extra long-distance charges.

One of the other ways of making long-distance calls is calling via the Internet. If the person you want to call has access to the Internet and has a microphone, conversations can be held easily with private voice chat rooms or instant-messaging provider, commonly known as PC-to-PC calls. But if the other person does not have access to a microphone or Internet, there are certain web sites that allow calling a person domestically through the Internet; there are, however, charges that apply. One thing to keep in mind, though, depending on your computer capacity and a few other technical issues, the quality of the calls may not be up to par with regular land-line service or calling card.

Making Small Daily Purchases

Do you buy a daily coffee from the local coffee store? Or, perhaps, a daily muffin from the bakery store? Or, perhaps, a daily chocolate bar from the vending machine? Although these may seem like a tiny amount spent every day, by the end of the month they add up to a larger figure than you may imagine. For example, assume your daily muffin costs $1.25. At the end of the workweek or school week, you've spent $6.25. At the end of a year, you've spent over $350! A good alternative to purchasing that one special item a day is to substitute it with something from home. For example:

- If you cannot live without that daily cup of coffee, you can always have it at home before you leave for school.
- If you cannot live without that cookie or muffin, make it yourself over the weekend and wrap it so you can easily grab it when heading out during the week.
- Consider getting a hard-plastic bottle for your water. You can easily boil or filter your tap water and refrigerate it, rather than buying bottled water.
- Seasonal fruits and vegetables can be very inexpensive snacks.

To overcome temptation of purchasing these little items, always have alternatives handy either in your bag or near you. Imagine saving $350 over a period of four years—you will have saved $1400.

Entertaining at Home

Having fun with your friends does not necessarily mean it will break your bank. It also does not mean that you have to leave your abode all the time either. There are ways of entertaining people and yourself with a small budget. We offer a few suggestions to get your mind thinking in this way:

- Have a potluck dinner. Have your friends prepare a dish each and you will have a cozy dinner party.
- Rent movies more often rather than going to the cinema. Also, find a local movie-rental store rather than the giant movie-rental store because the local stores often have better deals and prices.
- Host a murder-mystery night, which is different and rather inexpensive to do. It will keep your guests entertained all night.
- Throw a party where people will contribute some form of beverage or food to get into the party like an alternative way of having a cover charge.

• See an art exhibition or visit a museum with friends. As students, you benefit from a student rate. Classical or contemporary art exhibitions may be of interest or even your local science museum.

• Watch plays at the local theatres. You never know what kind of play you may stumble upon and how inexpensive it is.

• Check your city newspaper to see what's happening around your area in the arts and entertainment sections. Most of the major events such as festivals offer free admission.

• Watch a local band perform at a local venue.

• Watch for popular bands performing at a smaller venue rather than stadiums. Ticket prices for smaller venues tend to be lesser as well.

• Watch and listen for ticket information for popular bands performing on the same day.

• Participate in or attend events at your local community or student centres.

• For professional sporting events, most stadiums offer group discounts, host student nights, or have discount nights, so be sure to have a calendar of these events. But make sure you avoid stadium concession stands because the food tends to be highly marked up. (Bring your own snacks to save here.)

There are so many other things you and your friends can do, all you have to do is look around locally and have the initiative of organizing it. Throwing a dinner party is typically a tough task, especially the clean up. However, the money you save by not dining out or drinking at a club or bar can save you plenty. Hosting an event or organizing an event requires time, dedication, and participation from your friends. To create a successful event on a budget, you have to motivate your guests and friends to believe in your event. Their participation is key to the success of these events, no matter what the plan.

Video Rentals

If you like the "luxury" of home when doing your movie viewing—the comfortable couch an arm's reach from the fridge, and the power of the pause button locked in your hand—videos are a cheap way to go. We offer a few tips to make renting videos even cheaper:

- Take advantage of special nights. Video stores sometimes try to compete with theatres by offering deals such as "2-for-1 Tuesdays."
- Many video places offer promos such as every tenth movie free or a free movie on your birthday. Take advantage of these if you can.
- Avoid places that charge a membership fee unless it means guaranteed major savings.
- New releases sometimes cost more on weekends than during the week. You may want to rent these during the week and save older movies for the weekend.
- Try classics for a change. They're usually the cheapest to rent and there is a great selection, as other customers clamour after the latest releases.
- You're usually better off to go to a place where the selection is consistently good. That corner store may save you a buck or two, but if the selection is poor and you end up renting movies you wouldn't normally watch for free, you're really not saving.
- Avoid buying videos unless they're absolute classics. Most bought movies end their run sitting idly on your shelf.
- Unless your VCR doubles as a shredding machine, don't pay extra for the tape protection.

Video and CD Freebies

Rather than renting videos or compact discs at video and CD rental stores, borrow them from the library. They're free and the late charges are much cheaper.

Instead of renting videos or CDs, why not exchange ones you happen to own with friends or roommates?

Free music downloads abound on the Internet. While some are copyrighted material, there are plenty of free songs that can be downloaded legitimately. Enjoy the smorgasbord of legal material that's available as many bands, particularly the up-and-coming groups, sample their music on the Internet.

Along with videos, you may be able to rent CDs at a decent price as well. It's a great way to sample before you shell out for a "one-song-wonder" CD. Usually, rentals run from $1 to $2.

CD clubs have sprung up all over the place, luring you with the promise of low-cost music. "Any six CDs for 1¢." But be wary, by the time you buy the additional CDs, you are usually obligated to buy and pay shipping charges, making the cost creep up. Your individual cost per CD may be cheaper, but if you end up buying a lot more CDs than you normally would have, it's not a good deal overall. Be careful of getting involved with these clubs. Once you do, the flow of junk mail from them will hound you for years. Such advice also applies to video and book clubs.

If you're buying CDs or videos, the cheapest places are warehouse clubs (good prices, limited selection), electronic superstores (good prices, better selection), and music and video warehouse superstores (good prices, great selection). If you buy used, CD-exchange and resale stores offer some reasonable savings. Since CDs tend to stay in good condition, buying used is a safe option.

Reading Books

Entertainment may also include the calm relaxation of curling up with a good book—something that is not assigned for a change. Fortunately, there are some inexpensive options:

- The library is one of the best options. If they don't have it, they can probably get it for you, free of charge, from another library.
- If you've breezed through all your books and crave more, trade with roommates and friends. You'll get a taste of what other people read. If your roommates haven't yet graduated past the *Archie Comic* stage, you may want to check out a community book exchange.

• If you patronize one store, they may give you a frequent-reader card which entitles you to further discounts (while others may sell you one).

• Warehouse stores can give some great deals on current bestsellers—sometimes up to 50% off the cover price.

• For a cheap recycled read, a garage sale may be the ticket. Who knows what other people's libraries will provide?

• A great time to buy new books, including bestsellers, is January. Some books are half price, while many stores offer 15% to 20% off all selections. Stock up at this time.

Potluck Pleasures

Hosting a potluck dinner is a good way to entertain. Having each friend make one dish for dinner offers three big advantages: it's quick, cost-efficient, and filling. Potlucks take eating to the level of social entertainment, but with no pushy waiters, expensive menus, and annoying waits—just great company.

Campus Activities

One of the best parts of college and university is what you gain outside the classroom (not that you can't, of course, become a fountain of knowledge from what you learn inside the classroom). For more good times than you could ever imagine, consider the following very cheap opportunities:

• Most schools have a wide variety of clubs from ski and investment clubs to outdoor and Caribbean clubs. These are often free or charge minimal membership fees. The events they put on are often subsidized and therefore inexpensive. This is probably one of the absolute cheapest ways to meet people, have a good time, and learn something in the process.

• Student councils also offer a smorgasbord of programs, ranging from homecoming days to charity events. You've already paid for many of these activities through your student fees, so get your money's worth by participating.

For more academic entertainment freebies, we suggest you consider the following:

- If you've had enough of reading, let someone else do it for you. A variety of best-selling novelists and poets give readings on the campus circuit, hoping you'll be inspired enough to buy their books.
- Just what you needed, yet another lecture. But special lectures on campus are good and almost always free. Many renowned speakers, including entertainment and athletic figures, politicians, business leaders, social leaders, humanitarians, scientists, media figures, and so on, give lectures on campuses around the country. Your campus provides a venue for them—and cheap entertainment and information for you.

The Sporting Life—Playing Sports on Campus

If entertainment to you means staying away from the couch and venturing into some sort of sports complex, campus life can offer the discount route.

- You can usually learn and enjoy a sport through the recreation or physical education department or campus athletic clubs at a huge discount compared to what it would cost at a commercial facility. Fencing, scuba, and kayaking are just a few good examples.
- Campus athletic clubs often arrange deals with certain companies that offer cut-rate prices on athletic equipment. For example, squash racquets might be available at a 20% to 30% discount for squash-club members. You may have to pay a few bucks to join the club, but the savings could be worth it.
- Save money by purchasing your equipment at community sales or "replay" sports stores. If you have old equipment you don't use anymore, ask whether you can trade it in.

Quick tip: for athletic equipment, consider buying at equipment swaps on campus. Campus clubs, such as the ski club, often set up swaps and sales where you can pick up equipment at a fraction of the retail cost.

Armchair Athletics: A Sporting Gesture

If participation is not a word in your vocabulary but watching others work up a sweat is something you enjoy, you can take in some cheap sporting entertainment.

• Campus athletics offer great ways to see some top-notch athletics. Campus activities are often free or minimally priced for students.
• If your campus has excellent recreation facilities, your school may end up actually hosting national or even international meets by pro or Olympic teams. As a student, you can often get cheaper tickets for these events.
• Many cities have AAA and minor league teams, and tickets to see them compete are a fraction of the cost of professional sports.

Out on the Town

There are many ways to entertain yourself while living away from home and attending post-secondary studies. Whether you go to a movie, theatre, or a concert, there are various options available that can assist you in saving money.

Movies

• Check your on-campus theatre or film society for upcoming shows.
• Take advantage of mid-week cheap nights or matinees at commercial theatres when tickets are often half price.
• If a movie is awful, ask for your money back. Most theatres will give you a refund as long as you leave within the first half-hour of the movie.
• Check out second-run theatres, which usually charge several dollars less for movies that have been out for a couple of months.

- If you're sick of that same old formula: car chase + shootout = movie, try the repertory cinemas. These theatres often have great movies including limited-run films, international films, and cult classics. You'll usually pay less than at regular theatres. In addition, they frequently offer an annual membership, usually under $10, which will give you discounts on admission prices (and maybe even munchies!).

- Go for films that are especially good on the big screen. Save others, such as comedies, which will look just as good on TV, for when you can rent them from your local video store.

Munching at the Movies

If you think going to movies means getting robbed at the ticket booth, then you know that you'll also get mugged at the food counter. Movie theatres actually generate more profits from their refreshment booth than they do from admissions. To save money once inside the theatre, try the following strategies:

- Bring your own snacks to the cinema. You'll get a better selection at a fraction of the cost by bringing your own peanuts, chocolate bars, etc. While theatres don't promote this practice, it is allowed (unless otherwise posted) as long as you do not bring in any glass containers.

- If you buy beverages, order one large drink and an extra cup. You and your friend will have plenty to split at a fraction of the cost.

- Would you like pop with your ice? Ask them to hold off on the ice and give you more of the real stuff.

Broadway on a Budget

Live theatre is taking on a whole new popularity as people decide they'd like to do something in life other than gaze at TV and computer screens. But theatre can cost you big, with ticket prices on the major productions running between $75 to $100 or more. The following tips should help you avoid these hefty prices:

• Volunteer at a local community theatre. You will get to see some great shows, as well as pump up the resumé with volunteer experience.

• Take advantage of free or low-cost shows on campus. Drama departments and campus theatre groups offer some great productions at bare-bones prices.

• Take advantage of preview nights. Tickets are usually a lot cheaper for these shows, which run before the official opening night. So what if Romeo forgets Juliet's name a couple of times during the performance, it's still a great deal.

• Check out the alternative or underground theatres in your community, which often are both inexpensive and interesting.

If you're sampling professional or big-stage productions, try these tricks to avoid big-ticket prices:

• Ask for student rates and packages. The future of theatre depends on getting young people interested in this medium. Therefore, discounts offered to students are often "dramatic."

• "Rush" seats, last-minute no-shows, or unsold seats are usually sold off at a lower cost just prior to the performance. If you're prepared to go a bit early and take a chance, it's a good way to scoop up some savings. Some larger cities even have an outlet that just sells rush tickets for the various performances.

• Avoid Friday and Saturday evenings, which are usually more expensive.

• If you love the theatre but can't quite afford a season ticket, consider splitting a season ticket with friends. You can get the package discount without having to fork over for the whole bill of plays. Some theatres may even offer a discount "flex pass," which allows you to purchase tickets to a limited number of shows—say, four of the eight shows offered—and to choose the plays you want to see.

Comedy Clubs

If your roommates have lost their sense of humour, and even the class clown has lost his touch, you may be able to eke out a few laughs down at the comedy clubs. Stand-up comedy is popular, but the cost may wipe the smile right off your face. For cheap laughs, try the following tips:

• Take advantage of special student nights, which are sometimes half price.

• Some campus bars offer comedy that is so inexpensive it's a joke or even free.

• If you find watching stand-up humour too passive, remember there's always the chance to participate in amateur night when the cost is on them and the jokes are on you.

Concerts

It's always great to pay over $60 to hear some popular band; however, you can often pay a "song" for these concerts by choosing from the following strategies:

• If it's a show that is not sold out, you can sometimes pick up last-minute seats from the box office. Be careful with scalpers, since counterfeit tickets are common.

• If you think the average fan doesn't always get the best seats, you're right. Many of the tickets are held for radio stations and sponsoring companies. If you want front-row seats for the big show, your best bet may be through radio-show promotions or connections to big business. So turn on the radio and stick by the phone, or check with your parents, relatives, and friends to see if there are any spare box seats or front-row tickets floating around their companies.

• Some larger cities have ticket clearance outlets, which are a central box office for selling unsold last-minute seats. You can often get good seats at great prices here.

• Some ticket agencies tack costly service charges on top of regular ticket prices. Be aware of these extra fees and try to buy your tickets where the fees are not charged.

The list is endless. While you can't always do a lot, you may be able to cut down on these charges by buying from places like campus ticket outlets or directly from the theatre or concert-hall box office.

Other Concert Cost-Cutters

• If you can, hold off on buying the souvenirs. The markup is huge on concert merchandise and you'll probably find it at a lower cost in a retail store.

• If you buy food at concerts or other events at large concert halls and stadiums, you'll pay a fortune. Stock up on snacks before you go. While bringing potato chips may not win you many friends at the opera, packing a lunch for open-air concerts and sporting events saves you a bundle. Note that security at most concert halls and stadiums won't let you bring in alcohol or hard containers.

Free-for-Alls

• Look for free concerts, particularly during holidays and the warmer months. They are often promos sponsored by the beverage companies and local radio stations.

• There's free entertainment and it's loose in the streets! You can take in some amazing free festivals in towns and cities around the country, from the International Busker Festival in Halifax, the International Jazz Festival in Montreal, and the Home County Folk Festival in London, to Winterlude in Ottawa, Caribana in Toronto, and Klondike Days in Edmonton. Most of these festivals offer all or much of the entertainment for free. Drop by your local tourist bureau and enjoy.

• Check out the campus concert scene where you'll find some great up-and-coming bands that haven't quite made the big time—sort of like the AAA teams of the music world.

• If your school has a faculty of music, you may dig up some free concerts. While you're more likely to find classical or jazz than you would find techno punk, the quality is usually very good. And if you really want to mellow out, you may just want to saunter into a piano recital now and then.

Dating and Romance

When relationships start there are many ways to date without spending your entire entertainment and food budget:

- Try new and interesting things that don't cost money.
- Try simple things. Advertisers love to convince us that we need to spend lots of money to show our love and affection for someone. However, the simple (and inexpensive) things are often the most appreciated and remembered.
- Go for fun activities that will keep the laughter flowing.
- Be spontaneous. Sometimes the sudden or surprise things you do can be the most fun. Two is better than one.
- Take advantage of discounts for couples.

Here are eleven great student dates:

1. Go to a local beach or park and have a picnic.
2. Rent a favourite movie together and make your favourite munchies.
3. Take a trip to the local pet store and name all the animals or identify which celebrity or classmate they resemble.
4. Go tobogganing or cross-country skiing together and pack a lunch to share.
5. Have a Christmas wrapping party with the appropriate foods and beverages. Make the party complete with Christmas music and a holiday video such as *How the Grinch Stole Christmas*.
6. Make a big deal of other holidays too. For example, create a spooky scene for Halloween complete with carved pumpkins and costumes or plan a celebration of the Chinese New Year.
7. Take a fun class or course together and discover a new passion. Some things to try: Tai Chi, ballroom dancing, photography, fitness classes, massage courses, etc.
8. Volunteer to do some community work together. Everybody wins with this type of date.
9. If you're in the middle of mid-terms, turn an afternoon of

hitting the books into a pleasurable experience. Study in the park and bring a favourite game or Frisbee to take fun breaks.
10. If you don't already have one, borrow a dog to take for a long walk.
11. Do a crossword together.

Clothes Shopping

Depending on where you buy your clothing, the amounts can either be ridiculously cheap or astronomically expensive. Knowing the store can help you keep your money in your bank account. Finding out about store policies regarding price changes can help tremendously: most stores have policies about refunding the difference if there is a price change within a certain number of days. You should also find out about when the new collection will come in at stores because sometimes the store will mark down a few of the items in the current clothing line to make place for the new line.

Outlet stores are also a great place to shop as well; however, it is harder to keep up with current trends in some of the outlet stores. Purchase essential or classic pieces such as T-shirts or suits in outlet stores because they are considerably marked down. Keep in mind that clothes nowadays are made to be worn for at least three seasons or even up to two years before drastic fashion trends take over. Keep in mind:

• Depending on your style, you can easily accessorize the pieces you buy to make them more current and timeless as well.
• Make sure you are aware of the washing and maintenance procedure in order to keep your clothing in the best condition for the longest possible time.

Consider looking in the newspaper to see special manufacturer's sales on clothing as well: you can find current fashion trends for up to 80% off. Overall, when you are shopping for clothing, choose items that are versatile: pieces that can be worn a long time and that can be worn in any weather. If you have invested in expensive pieces in your wardrobe, you should keep them as long as possible because fashion trends are cyclical: styles and trends are often revived after a few years.

Travelling

If your budget allows you to travel abroad, you may want to try to minimize the cost while having maximum fun, depending on where your trip is located and the chosen transportation method. Check all possible outlets for price ranges and accommodations. The Internet offers a wide spectrum of sites that provide flight, accommodation, and package-deal prices. However, sometimes travel agencies can offer you a better deal. Things that you should keep in mind when planning to travel:

• Know which season it is you are travelling in. Is it a high-volume travelling season to that destination? Or is it the end season? Travelling to destinations where it is considered high season can cost much more for flights and accommodations; lower season typically offers you lower fares. However, make sure you compare both, whether it is for transportation or accommodation, because sometimes you can get a better deal in terms of services during high season.

• Be flexible in terms of dates for the trip. There is nothing wrong with planning your trip ahead of time. Sometimes you can get discounts if you plan your trip in advance; however, for those who are very flexible in terms of travelling, last-minute deals may be more suitable. Also, sometimes choosing an earlier or later departure or arrival date can save you plenty of money.

• Compare airfare of different airlines. Some airlines that specialize in certain destinations will provide better deals than other airlines.

Budget Travel Guides

So, you've just stepped off the plane; now what? These online travel guides will help you expand your knowledge and extend your dollar:

Arthur Frommer's Budget Travel Online (www.frommers.com)

Contains detailed information for cities worldwide.

Each entry lists the main attractions, accommodations, and local transportation.

Let's Go Online (www.letsgo.com)

The online version of the student travel series produced by Harvard University Press.

Find answers to your questions regarding travelling on a budget.

Lonely Planet Online (www.lonelyplanet.com)

This guide has a wealth of information for the budget traveller: health information, FAQs, myths, travelogues, and useful links.

Rough Guide Travel (travel.roughguides.com)

A comprehensive travel guide.

Yahoo! Travel (travel.yahoo.com)

Simple guides to hundreds of countries.

Excite Travel (travel.excite.com)

Check out this collection of travel and tourism information and links for Canadian cities, counties, and regions.

Becoming a Conscious Consumer

You can do many things now to guarantee you spend less and save more. Let's face it, there are plenty of things a person can do to save money. It is your willingness and motivation to do so that makes the difference. Some things that you can do are fairly easy, while others things may be more tedious. The following are things we recommend you do because they are easy to do and manage:

- Use less of everything. Use less hot water. Use less electricity. Use less toothpaste, shower gel, and cleaning products. Things we typically overuse are meant to be used in a certain way, such as cleaning products. Have you ever noticed that some liquid softeners need to be diluted? Also, a tiny amount of dish soap used in a sink full of water and dishes is as effective as putting your dish soap directly on a sponge. Bathroom cleaners should be left on for effectiveness before scrubbing. Hair conditioner should only be used at the lower end of your hair (bottom half of your head).

• Buy your food items in the grocery store and your other household products in discount retail stores.

• Make sure you evaluate purchasing household products in bulk versus buying it in singles. Sometimes buying in bulk is not as advantageous as you think. Calculators can come in handy in stores.

• Make sure you check your refrigerator on a daily basis to see which items are on the verge of spoilage and use them immediately.

• Buy generic products rather than brand-name products.

• Verify your receipts.

• Ask your friends or colleagues about services they use.

The following are things we recommend you do that are challenging but very worthwhile:

• Budget for food, entertaining, utilities, and extras.

• Maintain a record of what, when, and for how much you purchased your items.

• Scan weekly flyers for grocery or retail stores.

• Clip coupons, read the fine print, and make sure you use them before expiration.

• Keep your coupons organized.

• Plan and/or organize an entertaining event.

• Research companies, products, and alternatives.

• Cut down on vices such as smoking, drinking, and gambling.

Nobody ever said saving money was easy, but you should question yourself and justify your purchases in terms of your most basic needs. Carefully making the correct day-to-day decisions will only benefit you and your future financial plans. Becoming aware of what you buy and what you are paying for is key to cutting down on unnecessary costs.

Chapter Six
Credit

Now that you have decided which university to attend and where you will stay while attending, you are now left with the decision as to how you will be financing your studies. Some students will have registered education savings plans (RESP) set up for them by their parents. You may also have your own savings and may still have to work your way through—with part-time and/or summer employment.

In any event, students will probably have to take on debt at some point during the completion of their post-secondary education. There are many ways to take on debt, but students must make sure they do it for the right reasons and do it smartly.

Other than student loans, the two most common types of debt are lines of credit and credit cards. In this chapter, we will take a look at the differences between these as well as show students how expensive debt can become if it is not used intelligently. Moreover, it is very important to mention that if credit is used wisely, many doors could open to students in terms of their credit bureau, which we will also discuss in the course of this chapter. Basically, if students make use of their debt without getting carried away and by paying back all amounts and interest on time, it will be easier for them to eventually receive larger amounts of credit after graduating in order to purchase such items as their first car or even a first home.

Access to and intelligent use of credit is one of the most important aspects in a person's financial picture. After reading this chapter, students can make the optimal decision and choose to incur and manage debt wisely.

Credit and You

When you think of credit, you probably first think of plastic swipe cards, but there is more to credit than a piece of plastic. Credit offers many advantages, yet, used inappropriately, it can cause much strain. Your credit record follows you for life, so the choices you make in your post-secondary years can lead to either very good future benefits or potentially disastrous consequences. So, whether you're signing up for your first card, starting a cell-phone account, or shopping for a car, it is important to be informed about credit.

Benefits of Credit

Credit exists primarily to allow you to make an immediate purchase of an item for which you do not have the available cash at that moment. (The extension of this thought is that you will have the cash in the future and the expenditure is budgeted.) Cars and houses are common examples. There aren't many people walking the streets with a couple hundred thousand saved up in cash. Although the average college student is not concerned with buying a house, other items that have a useful life over a period of time (including a laptop or textbooks) are items that are commonly purchased on credit. In this manner, the payment for the good or service is "matched" with the actual usage of the item over an extended period.

Secondly, credit can provide a safety net. Suppose "Jim" knows he needs to buy a laptop in the near future for school. He can put aside a bit each week in a budget to buy the item with cash. However, what happens if Jim's current computer crashes the day before a paper is due? Will he have the money available in a pinch? Having credit can help you manage the risk of unexpected events. Many people purchase items on credit when travelling as it is safer than carrying large amounts of cash or travellers' cheques. On her trip to Mexico during spring break, "Claire" will not be a target to predators while she uses a credit card at a pool bar as opposed to having to hide a wallet full of cash under her towel.

Lastly, credit can also provide leverage to a consumer in dealings with a vendor. When "Steve" makes a purchase with credit, the seller must deliver in order to be paid. If the product isn't what was promised or has defects, Steve has recourse and an avenue to get his money back that a cash transaction with a disreputable vendor does not offer.

Besides the convenience, assurance, and gratification provided by credit, there are some additional advantages to using it wisely. Frequent-flyer and reward-point programs systems can lead to benefits beyond the purchased products but should not be the sole reason to use credit. Credit-card and debit-card statements are also useful in tracking how your spending compares to your budget, providing an item-by-item transaction record. Many credit-card issuers provide the capability to download transaction records directly into personal-finance software.

Drawbacks of Credit

For all of the positive attributes noted above, there are some drawbacks that you should be aware of:

- Interest expense
- Spending beyond your budget
- Privacy

Interest Expense

When using credit, there is an inherent cost of borrowing. There is no such thing in life as a free lunch, and there is no such thing as free money. Credit has its own terminology for the cost associated with it. One such cost is interest. Interest is the percentage that a lender charges for giving you use of its funds and is calculated as a percent of the borrowed amount for a stated period of time (day, month, and year). For example, let's say a credit facility charges interest at a rate of 1% per month. You multiply this rate by the number of periods in a year—you get what is called the annual percentage rate (APR). However, the APR can be misleading as it ignores compounding over the periods. The adjusted APR for compounding is called the periodic rate. Looking at the example of the credit card with an APR of 12%, here is a table showing the hidden cost of compounding based on the number of periods in a year:

Compounding Periods in a Year	APR	Periodic Rate
1 (annually)	12%	12%
4 (quarterly)	12%	12.56%
12 (monthly)	12%	12.68%
365 (daily)	12%	12.74%
Continuously for 1 year	12%	12.75%

Even though the APR for a credit facility is stated at 12%, if interest is calculated daily, the real interest rate is 0.74 of a percentage point higher. Keep in mind that some credit cards carry APRs as high as 24.99%, making the real interest rate of a daily-interest compounded card 28.39%. It should also be noted that most credit agreements are required to specify the basis on which the interest is calculated and charged and to disclose this to the customer.

Spending Beyond Your Budget

Credit can also lead to individuals making purchases they don't really need. You see ads all the time for goods with "no payments for one year." Not everyone needs a 42-inch plasma TV, but if you don't have to pay for a year, it seems like a deal, right? Nevertheless, in the end, people pay out much more than the TV cost for a product that instead of $2,500, they could get a basic 25-inch model for $250. This fuelling of consumption only serves to draw people into making purchases that they cannot afford.

This is a critical concept: credit is *not* free money! You eventually have to pay cash tomorrow for the purchases made on credit today. Using credit wisely means that you only use credit when you are certain that you will have that money tomorrow.

Privacy

Another drawback of credit is that it leads to an encroachment on your privacy. With all your personal information on file with a credit bureau, lenders can see where you live and work. Potential employers know if you owe court-ordered child-support payments or if the government is after you for back taxes. Your credit file is you, and many more people have access to it then you may realize.

We'll talk more about credit bureau records in a few pages, but in order for an entity (landlord, cellphone company, financial institution, etc.) to access your credit bureau record, they must have your authorization (usually through a signature on an application). You are encouraged to thoroughly read any "applications" (or similar items) that you are asked to fill out. The application should specify what authority you are giving to the organization to review your credit. Sometimes it's a "one-time" authorization, but it can often give the user ongoing access. Their access is typically ended when the account is closed and all outstanding balances are paid in full.

Finally, pay your bills! Even minuscule amounts can be considered as "unpaid" and can create a black stain on an otherwise excellent credit record.

Types of Credit

There are different forms of credit that are commonplace: secured, unsecured, and guaranteed. Secured credit is granted when you provide security or collateral against the loan. With this type, if you default on your loan (stop making payments), the lender will "cash in" or liquidate the security and thus get the loan paid off (or reduce the amount owing). Examples of security could be savings bonds or Guaranteed Investment Certificates (GICs)—these are considered excellent security, as they rarely lose value. With this type of security, you give the financing company the actual certificates and they hold onto them until the loan is paid off in full. You could expect to get 100% loan value. In other words, if you put up $5,000 in bonds, you would get a $5,000 loan (usually at a very competitive rate like prime rate). Another form of secured lending would be a car loan, where the car itself is the security for the loan. In this case, you would not likely get a loan for the value of the car, instead only a portion—typically 50% to 75% of the value of the auto. This is because cars lose value quite quickly, can be stolen, or lose complete value as a result of an accident.

Unsecured

With unsecured credit, lenders have no guarantee that you will repay other than your promise to do so. This is the case with most major credit cards. They can take you to a collection agency in addition to enacting stiff penalties for failure to pay, including raising your interest rate, lowering your credit limit (the maximum amount you can borrow), and cancelling your account.

Co-Signed (Guaranteed) Loan

A co-signed loan is where the borrower has another person "guarantee" a loan. This is typically a parent, but can be anyone (aunt, uncle, grandparent, sibling, friend, etc.), and must be someone who knows you well. With this type of loan, the co-signer guarantees that they will repay the loan if you do not. This provides the lender (the bank or other type of financial institution) with an additional layer of comfort because the co-signer is typically a very creditworthy individual and they add strength to your credit submission.

Generally speaking, a secured loan could have a lower interest rate than a co-signed loan, and, lastly, an unsecured loan would have the highest rate. This is because the lender has additional opportunity to recover the money owed and compensates for this with reduced interest rates. Normally, the lower the risk to the lender the lower the rate to the borrower.

Most students, if they had $5,000 available, would likely use it to pay for their expenses, as opposed to putting it up as security or collateral, so these types of loans are very uncommon with students. Co-signed loans are very typical with lines of credit and credit cards are very common examples of an unsecured loan.

The type of credit you have entered into when you get a credit card or loan will be written out in the loan agreement. It is important to fully read and understand the contract language before you use the card or loan. Your use will signal acceptance and understanding of the terms and conditions stated, leaving you little recourse if you do not fully understand.

Credit Bureaus & Your Credit Record

All of your personal information required by a lender is kept in your credit file. Your credit history is like your favourite sweatshirt—it'll stay with you long after you first got it. It will show that coffee stain on the front, the pull on the side, and the fraying collar no matter how hard you scrub, stitch, and line dry. Just as you would not subject your sweatshirt to harsh bleaching, you must also take care of your credit history. Credit, unlike that favourite sweatshirt, doesn't come with a care label. But, like cotton, there are certain things you must do and others that you should avoid.

Your credit record is stored in information clearing houses. The "Big 3"—TRW, Equifax, and TransUnion—are the most commonly used and referred to when discussing credit. They will each keep a personal file on you. Each time you fill out a credit application, the information on it is updated in your credit file. This information contains your name, social security/insurance number, current and previous address, as well as current and previous employer.

Also contained in the file is your credit history. This is a record of all your existing credit accounts. A credit-bureau check is "run" when the information is requested from a clearing house; all current balances will be shown as well as payment history. For example, your MasterCard account may appear like this:

Name: MasterCard
Type: Credit Card

(2/99) Limit: $2,000	30–60	60–90	90–120	120+
Current Balance (3/7/05):	2	0	0	0

$178
Status: Current

This means on your account, you owe $178 on your bill due March 7, 2005. It shows your credit limit of $2,000 as well as the fact that you've had the account since February of 1999. The type of account is listed; in this case, it's a credit card. It also shows that you've been 30–60 days past due on two occasions within seven years. At the end, it states that your account is current, meaning that payments on your account are up to date (i.e. you have made the requested minimum payment on or before the monthly account cut-off date).

If your credit history with this lender was not so good, your record may appear in the bureau like this:

Name: MasterCard
Type: Credit Card

(2/99) Limit: $2,000	30–60	60–90	90–120	120+
Current Balance (10/7/04): 7		4	2	1

$578
Status: Collection

This report will tell a prospective lender that you owe $578 on your card, dating back to October of 2004. It also shows that you've been late a total of fourteen times—seven times over one month, four times over two, and two times you went more than ninety days after your billing date before paying. It also states that to reclaim its losses, the creditor has taken you to collection. An entry like this on your credit file can instantly cost you a loan.

Also included on a credit file are things of public record. For example, if the city has filed a lien for property taxes or if you have failed to make court-ordered child-support payments, it'll appear on your credit file. While this is not likely to be a concern for students, it does demonstrate the extent of information that can be contained on a credit record.

Also shown is any recent activity on your bureau record. For six months, every time a lender runs your bureau, it shows on the file. For example, you go to shop for a new car and you fill out a credit application at a dealership. If you also fill out applications at other dealerships, the successive dealers will see that you are shopping them. Here's the rub: if you have been to multiple dealers, an astute manager will recognize that in most cases this may be due to an inability to obtain financing, which could alter the way a sales rep works with you. This potentially affects not only the purchase price but also the financing interest rate as well. The lesson here is that multiple "hits" on the credit bureaus can alert lenders to your situation and, although a privacy incursion, may limit your negotiating power and potentially reduces your overall perceived creditworthiness.

What Is a Credit Score?

Keep in mind the credit bureaus have records for tens of millions of people and they have developed very sophisticated statistical models. Essentially, they look at the credit usage and payment behaviours and characteristics of people who have defaulted on loans and/or gone bankrupt (compared with those whose records are "clean") and render a "score." Lenders will use these scores to help assess your creditworthiness. They would typically be used as part of a decision of whether or not they will grant credit. It also considers such factors as how much credit to grant, the interest rate, minimum payment requirements, and the lending product(s) that you may or may not qualify for. In other words, your credit score is a widely used tool by lenders, and all your credit usage and payment behavior will either raise (better credit risk) or lower (worse credit risk) your score. Lenders will have access to your score over time as well so they will look for a trend line. For example, if your current score is "middle of the road" but has shown improvement over the past twelve to twenty-four months, this would demonstrate the you are improving your ability to manage your personal finances and to service your debts.

Managing Your Credit Record

All active accounts will appear on your credit file. An inactive account will remain for up to eleven years. Public-records information remains for seven years and bankruptcies are removed after ten years. However, because of the length of time a record stays on your bureau, it is important to check your credit bureau periodically by contacting one of the major clearing houses. This is extremely important, as an estimated 20% of credit files contain errors serious enough to warrant credit being declined.

Credit and Post-Secondary Education

In this next section, we will examine two typical credit instruments that are very commonly used by students: lines of credit and credit cards.

What Is a Line of Credit?

A line of credit (also known as a credit line) is a lending instrument that generally has the following characteristics:

• Has a defined limit and is "perpetual": The "limit" identifies the maximum amount you can borrow (i.e. $10,000). Unlike personal loans that have a term or time frame on them, lines of credit do not expire as long as you are in good standing with your financial situation and you are not experiencing any debt-related problems. Because of its perpetual nature, you do not have to reapply every time you need money. Plus, when you pay down the balance, you "reopen" the credit line and can "re-borrow." Basically, you can have access to the limit of the line over and over again, like a revolving door, without exceeding the limit. In this manner, a line of credit provides you with a great deal of flexibility to manage your finances and debt obligations.

• Payment flexibility: The line of credit will have a defined monthly repayment amount—interest only, 1% to 3% of balance, minimum of $50, etc., so you can manage your payments. In one month, you could pay off $1,000 and the next month, only $100.

• Interest rates: The line of credit could have a "floating" interest rate, usually based on prime rate (i.e. prime plus 1.5%). One potential drawback could be the fact that credit line interest rates depend on the prime rate, which can fluctuate up or down at any time. In recent years, the prime rate has been as low as 3.75% and as high as 7.75%. As of summer 2005, the prime rate was 4.25%. In other words, the interest rate paid is never fixed unlike a personal loan where interest rates are guaranteed until the end of the term. However, it rarely happens that the interest rates on lines of credit exceed those paid on personal loans.

• Interest charges: A major benefit of credit lines includes the fact that you only pay interest on the amount borrowed. For example, say you were accepted for a $10,000 credit line, but you only need $1,000. In this case, you will only pay interest on the $1,000 you use. This means that having a credit line would cost you nothing if you never actually borrow (advance funds) from the line. You can have a line of credit set up simply in case of emergencies.

• How do you get (advance) the money? Lines of credit generally issue paper cheques to access the line. In addition, they are now often "linked" to your ATM card and can also be advanced through telephone and online banking. Some institutions will also issue a credit card that is linked to the line of credit. Please note: if you use these credit cards, you will be charged interest on the purchases immediately! (More on this in the credit-card section.)

Types of Credit Lines

There are two main types of lines of credit offered by banks specifically for students. We will discuss only student lines of credit since they will always offer better interest rates. The two types are:

• Credit lines for students, and
• Credit lines for students pursuing a professional designation. (Check with your bank to see if you qualify.)

The main difference is that those students pursuing professional designations are usually older and may already have significant financial obligations (car loans, mortgages, etc.). Second, they may have significant expenses related to their studies. For example, a dentistry student will have to buy their tools of the trade while still in university and these items can be very expensive. Third, the length of time before they begin to earn a regular income necessitates a different lending arrangement. Finally, because of the intensive nature of the studies, the students are unlikely to work part-time and during summers, so they require even more financial support for their living expenses.

How Do Credit Lines Work?

The major differences between the two types of student lines of credit are the "annual amounts" and the total amount that will be granted. A student line (regular or professional) typically has an annual amount and a total (maximum) amount. For example, a regular line will advance up to $10,000 per school year with a maximum of $40,000, while dentistry students could access $30,000 per year up to $120,000. These amounts may vary according to the lender and the borrower's debt-servicing capacity.

Professional lines generally have a lower interest rate versus the regular student line. With both types, you are generally required to pay interest only while in school and up to one year after you finish. After the one-year period, payments will be adjusted to reflect the interest and principal amounts.

It is important to note that banks will more often than not give you higher limits than you actually need, especially for students pursuing a professional designation. The goal of this credit line is to get you through university to a job that will help you repay the amount borrowed as quickly as possible, not to bury you under piles of debt and interest. So before you apply for a credit line, you must calculate how much credit you will need and then apply for that amount. The financial institution will advise you how much you qualify for. If they provide more than what you applied for, you may wish to be cautious in accepting the extra amount. You don't want to overextend yourself and have a heavy burden upon graduation.

Furthermore, with these lines of credit, each year you will be required to apply for the "new" funds, so the amount you are approved for may vary by year. Finally, each financial institution will have rules if you leave school early or decide to take a break for a year or two. You should ask for their specific rules on these types of situations.

Credit Cards

Credit cards are a common sight on college and university campuses. In the U.S., over 66% of undergraduate students have a credit card and 25% have more than four credit cards. The process of applying for a credit card is similar to that of a loan. The reference check is not as extensive. The same formulas and rules apply, however, in determining your line of credit and the maximum amount you can borrow. There are two types of cards that are most commonly available to students:

- "store" & "gas" cards (The Bay, Home Depot, Walmart, etc.)
- general credit cards (Visa, MasterCard, American Express)

Store & Gas Cards

These types of credit cards are limited for use only in the issuing store. They typically have a much higher interest rate than general credit cards, and lower credit limits as well. Store cards are often used to provide special discounts (i.e. save an extra 10% when you use your store card). They can often be used as a financing incentive as well (i.e. no interest or payments for ninety days on a minimum $300 purchase). In this manner, they do provide distinct benefits to the cardholder. However, these types of cards are becoming less available. For instance, both Canadian Tire and Sears have stopped issuing their store cards and now issue store-branded MasterCards. Many of the retail stores offer incentives such as points when customers use their brand of cards. These points accumulate and can be used to buy products from the store's point catalogue. A very good example of this is the HBC points, which ties into Zellers and The Bay.

Select gas retailers also have their own cards, but, again, these are a dwindling breed. The "big three" gas retailers in Canada have all migrated to general cards: Petro-Canada and Shell with MasterCard, and Esso with Visa. These cards are now starting to offer rebates per litre purchased (2¢ per litre is a recent offer by one of the larger gas retailers).

General Credit Cards

These cards are widely accepted at millions of merchants and also allow you to take cash advances at banks and ATMs. A credit card is designed to be a payment mechanism first and a borrowing device second. When approved, you are granted a limit (they are very similar to a line of credit in this respect) and are issued a plastic card—this is the card used at merchants.

Student cards are available to individuals attending or planning to attend college or university. They come with low-credit limits, typically around $500; many are "no-fee," but some may carry an annual fee up to $20 a year.

Card Features

Compared to other types of loans, credit cards usually have a lower credit limit and significantly higher interest rates. They can offer a variety of "perks" such as reward points, insurance protection, etc., and some carry annual fees. Furthermore, there are different levels of cards from basic cards to "gold" and "platinum" cards with higher annual fees but more features. However, as a student, don't pay more for a gold, platinum, or plutonium card if you won't utilize the features regularly. We recommend you ask about the added features before you pay the extra annual fees.

Interest Rates

As mentioned above, the rates can be quite high—18% to 20% APR is not unusual. Interest rates are declared for both cash advances and purchases—they are usually the same rate, but can be different. Also, some issuers will give you the option to get a low-rate (9% to 11% interest rate) card for an annual fee of $15 to $35.

Billings & Payments

The bills come at regular (usually monthly) intervals and will require a minimum payment—typically 2% to 5% of the balance owing with a minimum of $10 to $25.

Cash Advances

Most credit cards will also allow you to make cash advances at a bank branch or through an ATM. But please note: when you take a cash advance, you are charged interest immediately on that advance.

Grace Period

There is a nifty feature of credit cards which makes them different from other forms of credit and can save you from interest charges. It's called the grace period. The grace period is a specified time from when a purchase is made until when interest is calculated and added to the invoice amount. On most cards, the grace period ranges from seventeen to twenty-six days after your statement date. (On some cards, it can be as short as the next day—this is where the plastic card is actually linked to a line of credit and is not a true credit card.) It is important to understand the fine print on your card agreement as it specifies the grace period. If used properly, it can be like free money.

If you make the payment in full on the due date, you will pay no interest—effectively getting "free money" for the days leading up to the statement date from the date of purchase. Simple as that! You should pay the entire statement balance, in full, on or before the payment due date. If you don't, you effectively waive the grace day provision and will pay interest back to the original date of the transaction. Each issuer will have their own rules. Some will say that if you have *any* interest-bearing balance (cash advance, previous purchases), then there is no grace period on any new purchases. Read your cardholder agreement very carefully. If you have questions, call the card issuer for an explanation.

Affinity Cards

Affinity cards are commonplace on campuses. With these cards, the issuer will pay the school a percentage of the spending that occurs on the cards. (Even though the amount is very small—usually less than 20¢ per $100 of usage—there are millions of dollars being spent each month, so it can add up in a hurry!) For the student, they get to support their school and can be proud to use the card since the plastic itself showcases the school name, crest, and a photo of a campus landmark. While the "charity" side of the card may be appealing, you should ensure that the card has all the features and benefits that you require.

Balance Transfers

Issuers will try to entice you to transfer a balance with a "low introductory rate" (i.e. pay 2.9% for six months). While this may be a very attractive rate, consider a few things:

- At the end of the six months, your interest rate will go up to the regular rate in the higher range which could be more than 18%.
- If you make purchases on the card, they will get interest charges at the higher declared rate (assuming you don't pay the entire balance in full).
- Payments are deducted from the lowest interest-rate balance—you will pay off the 2.9% balance and get interest charges on the 18% balance.

If you are going to take advantage of the introductory rate, avoid using the card for any other transactions—this way, you will preserve the balance at the low rate. Also, if you are late or miss a payment, the card issuer may cancel the low rate and put you at the regular interest rate.

Reducing (Eliminating) Interest Charges

Besides the APR discussed previously, there is another important aspect of credit cards to understand: do not buy items that you cannot pay for now with cash. This is a hard lesson to learn and over time, you will see the benefit of this golden rule. The interest you'll pay on credit-card balances is much higher than conventional loans, so you should try to avoid carrying a balance whenever possible. However, if you find you are persistently carrying a balance and paying interest, the "low rate" feature discussed above may be an excellent alternative. Furthermore, if you have both a credit card and a line of credit, it is probably best to pay off the credit card in full and carry the balance on your lower-rate line of credit. A very good rule of thumb for any credit is to always pay off higher-cost debt first. Your interest savings over time can be quite extensive.

Working with Your Credit-Card Issuer

Another aspect that is not commonly known is that you can negotiate with credit-card companies. If your card issuer charges an annual fee, call and ask if it can be waived. This commonly works and even more so for students. Tell them you will take your business elsewhere (and be ready to support your claim) and the credit-card companies will usually support your request. The same leverage works if your payment arrives a few days late. If you are a good customer with a history of making payments on time, the companies will usually waive the interest charges and/or other fees. This does not mean that you can be late every month, but accidents happen. Maybe you forgot to get stamps and then it was the weekend and your payment couldn't go out until Tuesday morning. That happens; and for good customers, the credit companies will be accommodating. A friendly phone call will usually do the trick. But like credit, goodwill is not something that should be abused, only to be used when needed. Don't be late too often as this will show up on your credit bureau.

Creating & Building Your Credit Profile

Credit cards are a common sight on college campuses. With so many students possessing credit cards when they set foot on college campuses, it is very important that they understand how their credit will affect them after university.

There are many rumours circulating about how to build credit. A cellphone or house phone is an easy place to start. Usually, to get a house phone, you must place a substantial deposit with the phone company. This is to guard against the risk of default when you have no credit history. After six months, if all bills are paid, the deposit is usually refunded since a credit history has been established. (Remember, the phone companies are part of the credit bureau "network.")

Another method of building credit is to sign up for a credit card. A student card is a great place to start. Now with a credit card, there are two mindsets on how to build your credit. One school of thought says you should carry a balance month to month, making just the minimum payment to show that you are responsibly managing your finances. Another thought is that the balance should immediately be paid off, also believing that this shows fiscal responsibility. There is no correct method, but do one or the other and, as mentioned earlier, don't be late. Having said that, here's a golden rule:

You should always make at least the minimum payment by the due date.

Do that, and you will build a good credit record. Here's something else to know: people who pay the balance in full generally have a higher credit "score" than those who carry a balance!

You should use your card, but don't over use it. After six months, you should consider applying for a credit-limit increase and if you only have a store card, apply for a major-brand (MasterCard, Visa, or American Express) credit card, further building your credit history. The most important aspect to take away from this is that using your card and making payments builds credit experience. Inactivity and missed payments lowers your credit score, making you less appealing to lenders.

Housing and Employment

Living out on your own can be fun and exciting. Credit allows it to happen. When you enter into a rental agreement, the landlord has the right to check your credit history. Your credit is, in a sense, a form of reference. If you have a poor credit history, including failure to pay bills on time, the landlord may reject your application. There is nothing worse than finding that needle in the haystack apartment and finding out you cannot move in to it.

Your credit history may be important when you look for employment. To handle money and become bonded (i.e. when employed at a financial institution) you cannot have any bankruptcies on your credit file. Also, employers in the U.S. are beginning to check credit. According to Sarah Snyder's article "Indebted students beware: employers checking credit," published in the *Lantern*, Ohio State University's newspaper, anybody who handles or may handle money, from salespersons to delivery drivers, are finding themselves subjected to credit checks. What you may find is that employers are treating credit history as an indicator of your character. The idea is that if you are in financial difficulties, you have a higher likelihood of stealing and/or failing to perform on the job. If there are numerous external pressures placed on you, there's the risk of mental distraction at work, which would lead to diminished performance and corrupted morals.

I've Gotten in Over My Head—What Should I Do?

Many credit-counselling services provide free and low-cost help at getting you out of debt (www.nfcc.org). These services will work with creditors to reduce your monthly payments, thus reducing your debt load. The creditors are willing to do this as it is better for them to get a little back at a time as opposed to you declaring bankruptcy and risk not seeing a single penny from you. However, do not use these credit-counselling services as a way to accumulate more debt. These services are a last resort. They are not an excuse for credit misuse. Some of these services offer resources on budgeting- and credit-education seminars. Only trust the non-profit centres as many of them are funded by governments—local, provincial, or federal. The logic behind this is simple economics: bankrupt individuals cannot purchase as many goods and services as those with credit. The purchases of goods and services reflect the health of the economy, giving the government an interest in keeping you out of bankruptcy.

Using Credit Wisely
Loans

So you found a great car and you really want it but you don't have the cash to pay for it in full. Well, no problem—get a loan! But before you sign on any dotted line, there are a few things you need to consider before applying.

- How much you really need to borrow: This seems simple enough, but don't forget some hidden costs such as insurance and registration. In some jurisdictions, if you are financing an automobile, you are required to carry collision insurance and until you make the last payment, the vehicle is technically not yours.

• Length of repayment: Longer periods reduce monthly payments but increase the interest amount you have to pay. You need to find the right balance for you. Ask to see all options and see which ones match your budget. "Don't just take the salesman's word on it," is the advice coming from one former car dealer.

• Method of repayment: Are you going to repay the entire loan at maturity or in installments? Again, look at all the options and decide what is best for you. For smaller items, a lump-sum payment may be the best option. For an automobile, installments or possibly a hybrid option (sometimes called a balloon payment whereby you make monthly installments and after forty-eight months you pay off the remaining balance) usually work best.

• Assets you own: If you can make a down payment, do it. It drastically reduces your monthly payments since the amount borrowed, the principal, is much less, as are the interest charges. Vehicle trade-ins can usually be counted towards a down payment.

• What the bank will ask from you: Pay stubs, tax returns, sources of deposits (bank statements, etc.), proof of residency, and insurance will be asked of you by lenders in the automobile business. Many other lenders will seek similar items. Have them handy or readily available when applying for a loan.

• Shop around: Be prepared to work to get the best deal. Keep an eye on the newspapers to follow the going rates. It is good to have a history with a particular lender, but do not be married to them.

The Credit Process & Application

In evaluating a candidate for a loan, lenders try to predetermine one's ability to repay the money borrowed in the terms established. Their criteria are summed up by the "Three Cs of Credit: Character, Capacity, and Collateral." Each is explained in the following discussion of the credit application, the first step to getting a loan.

There is a science behind the awarding of loans as a lender

attempts to evaluate the risk of a lending candidate. This process is referred to as the credit application, or, for short, the credit app. The credit app will require some basic biographical information, starting with the applicant's name. Married women have a choice in this aspect. A woman can use her maiden name, her assumed surname, or a hyphenated merger of the two. The loan process is much simpler if the same name that appears on tax filings, pay stubs, and utility bills are used. A social insurance number (SIN) also simplifies the process, as it is a unique personal tag. It has been said that the SIN is not required to process a credit app, but based upon the experience of our credit expert, Graham McWaters, it is impossible to do a credit check on an applicant without their SIN.

The credit app will also require information of the applicant's residence. The address is needed as well as tenure in the dwelling. A steady residency in one location is more appealing to a lender as it demonstrates stability, part of the character aspect. This is not to say moving is ill advised. However, frequent moving may lead to a loan being denied or the raising of the interest rate. In addition to where the applicant lives and for how long, an applicant must also disclose how much is paid monthly in either rent or mortgage payments. The applicant will also be asked to declare any and all loans, lines of credit, credit cards that they may have at that time, the lender wanting to evaluate the limit, monthly payments, and current balances.

A lender must be certain that you can pay back the loan. The credit app will inquire about your employment history. Not only must you provide the job you perform and your pay but you also may be required to include your supervisor's name and contact information as well as the address of the business. The latter is matched in the credit bureau's records against records on that business to determine if it even exists. You may also be asked to provide a recent pay stub to validate your employment and income. In addition, you may be asked to provide the prior year's Income Tax Notice of Assessments or T4 slips. Your supervisor may be contacted as a personal reference to help determine your character. On smaller loans, this is not common but does occur with greater frequency as the value of the loan increases. Lastly, the loan app will ask for the reason for the loan.

Lending "Adjudication"

With all of the information provided, plus additional information from the credit bureau report, the lender will evaluate your creditworthiness. This process is called adjudication and it works as follows:

Using your income documentation, the lender calculates your disposable income. They take your earnings, deduct for taxes, and then subtract your housing expenses. A lender may also deduct a percentage of that difference for things such as food and utilities. This formula leaves the lender with a rough calculation of your disposable income, or the amount of money you can freely spend. They then look at the amount you wish to borrow and how it relates proportionately to your disposable income. It is vital that the loan amount does not constitute a significant portion of disposable income. If any unforeseen events were to occur, like the loss of employment, the lender needs to know that the loan can be repaid. The higher the percentage of disposable income required for a loan payment, the higher the risk of defaulting and the less likely a lender will offer you the loan.

Whereas your pay helps clarify your capacity to repay the loan and is very straightforward, your length of time in a job and your employment history is used to determine character. As with frequent moving, job-hopping is viewed as an unfavourable trait, demonstrating instability and other character flaws. For instance, "Brendan" is applying for a car loan. He found a new car at the dealer and the payment is $270 per month. Brendan is employed part-time during the school year and works full-time in the summer, earning an average of $500 per week. He has been at his job for two years and the loan manager has heard nothing but positive comments about Brendan. Brendan lives at home and commutes to school. Tuition for him is $7000 per year. Ignoring his credit history for the time being, this is how his credit app would be evaluated:

$2000	Monthly earnings
- 400	Taxes at rate of 20%
0	Housing expense
1600	Disposable income
- 585	School expense per month
$1015	Available monthly income

The car loan of $270 represents a little over 26% of Brendan's income. Assuming a normal credit history, Brendan will likely get the loan. However, if Brendan had to pay $400 per month in rent, the picture would be more like this:

$2000	Monthly earnings
- 400	Taxes at rate of 20%
- 400	Housing expense
1200	Disposable income
- 585	School expense per month
$615	Available monthly income

Now the car payment represents 45% of Brendan's income. Most banks try to keep this ratio under 30%. On rare occasions, it is stretched to 40%, but it is highly unlikely that a bank would give Brendan this loan now.

There are alternative financing companies, however, that may be prepared to lend to Brendan but they will do so at very high interest rates. These rates may be as much as double or even triple the regular bank rate. You should be very cautious in dealing with these companies. But if you do, try to ensure there are no or minimal penalties for early payments so that you can pay off the higher interest-rate loan more quickly.

This is a brief overview of the lending process. Each lending institution has their specific policies and procedures. You are encouraged to always be honest in your dealings with a lender as anything less may cast suspicion upon you and reduce the likelihood of being approved for a loan.

In summary, here are a few concepts to keep in mind:

- Credit is a great resource, but don't become dependent on it.
- There are different types of credit because there are different types of people. You have to find the combination of factors that works best for you.
- Don't be afraid to ask for clarification or object to something. First off, you will not be laughed at. No one is born understanding credit. Secondly, it is your future; you have to ask because it matters most to you.
- Do your homework. Shop around and don't jump on the first offer.
- It is better to make the minimum payment than no payment at all, and it's best not to carry a balance.
- Just because something exists, it does not mean you need it. Only spend money that you actually have or that you will have when the payment is due!
- Mistakes happen, accidents happen. They are not the end of the world so be pro-active in dealing with the lender.

Chapter Seven
Getting a Job

You've survived college or university. Congratulations. It's now time to enter the real world. It's time to find your first job. But where do you start? There are probably a lot of questions running through your head: What can I do with my degree? What do I want to do with my degree? How do I start the job hunt? Where do I start the job hunt? What about a resumé? These are questions that every graduating student asks themselves. This chapter's goal is to help you answer these questions. It will guide you through the job process from determining what you actually want to do to accepting a job offer.

Determining the Careers That Are Right for You

It is a daunting task trying to figure out what you want to do with your degree once you graduate. There are some majors that lead directly to a specific career, such as marketing or civil engineering, and there are others that provide far less direction. No matter what your major is, however, you should not limit yourself. Every degree or diploma opens up doors in many different fields. For example, a student studying computer science may assume that their studies will lead to a job in IT, but the careers related to this major are widely ranging from computer scientists to teachers to risk and insurance specialists. How do you determine the right career for you? You first need to know yourself and then you need to understand the job market.

Know Yourself

The first step in preparing for employment is knowing yourself inside and out. What are your strengths, weaknesses, preferences, skills, interests, and values? What is your personality type? By truly understanding and recognizing these aspects of yourself, you will be able to determine who you are, what you want, and where you want to be.

To help you begin the introspection process, it is best to start by really getting to know yourself. It is important to not only understand who you are in the present but also to understand yourself in the past and the future. It is useful to take the time and write a short autobiography. In it, answer these three fundamental questions:

- Who are you?
- What has made you the person that you are?
- What are your goals in the short term (the next year), the medium term (the next two to five years), and the long term (five years and beyond)?

Take your time when answering these questions. Try to understand the meanings and reasons behind your answers. A useful method for doing this is known as the "five whys." In this method, for every descriptive statement you make, ask yourself "Why is that important?" five times. After you have answered the whys a few times, you will start to really understand what makes you tick. It is also important not to limit your answers to what you think would be career related but to expand them into every aspect of your life. By doing this, you will be far more successful in determining what career path is right for you.

Once you have taken the time to analyze who you really are, you need to establish what kind of work environment is ideal for you. To begin this process, start by answering the questions in Figure 1 of the appendices. Remember that there are no right or wrong answers to these questions. If you do not like working in a team setting or it is important that you have a high salary, that is fine. What would not be fine is lying to yourself and ending up in a job or a career that you don't like.

You can use many other tools for self-assessment. Your career-services centre has many tools to help you assess your qualities and characteristics. A career counsellor is trained to assist you in this process and most career centres have tests that can help you with the introspective process. You could also surf the net for career aptitude and personality tests. The Government of Canada's Job Futures web site (jobfutures.ca) has an excellent quiz that can help you to determine which careers are best suited to you.

Know the Job Market

The next step in determining which careers may be right for you is to understand the job market you will be entering. You have to be able to make realistic decisions about your career and where you are headed. To do this, you have to recognize the opportunities and limitations that the current and future markets have. When your parents first entered the workforce, it was expected that the job and career you started after graduation would be what you would have for the rest of your life or most of it. Today, a new university graduate can expect to switch jobs between eight and ten times and have up to three different careers during his or her lifetime.

The key to understanding the job market and what potential careers are out there for you is research, research, and more research. The Government of Canada lists over two hundred twenty-six occupational groups in the labour market. It is important to understand which of these many jobs have good prospects in the future and which do not. Understanding the job market thoroughly will also help you to identify which careers complement your interests and qualifications as well as which areas you need to improve if you would like to enter a particular field. There are several different tools you can use when gathering career data. Good places to start your research include:

- Your campus career centre: This is an excellent resource for information on different occupations and it provides tools to determine which careers are right for you.
- The World Wide Web: The Internet is a vast resource for

information on the job markets. If you are interested in careers abroad, it is probably the most accessible resource you have to find information on the workforces in different countries as well as the requirements they have if you wish to work there. Figure 9 lists several web sites that provide career-planning information and resources.

• Libraries: There are many print resources dedicated to providing information about the job market. For instance, many national magazines publish special annual issues that examine the workforce (i.e. *Maclean's*).

Other useful ways to learn about a particular field include taking a summer job, internship, part-time job, interviewing someone who works in the field, monitoring the classified ads to learn more about the field, and joining professional organizations in the field. These tactics help you to learn more about the field and gain valuable information about that field such as skills required, what you would actually do in a particular job, and what the opportunities are in the given field.

The purpose of all this research is not to narrow your career goals down to one option but instead to help you to identify several careers that interest you and that you are suited for. It will also help you in the rest of the employment process. If you have not completed these two steps, it is far less likely that you will be successful in finding a job that suits you and you will be successful in. Knowing yourself and understanding the job market can assist you prior to going on the job hunt.

The Job Hunt

By now, you know what field you are interested in pursuing a career in. It is now time to start the actual job hunt. Students often fall into the habit of using the most traditional methods for job hunting such as replying to classifieds or relying on your campus career centre. To be a successful job seeker, you cannot rely on only one or two methods. Remember: if you simply do what everyone else is doing to search for jobs, you reduce your chances of getting the job you really want. You can use many different techniques when searching for a job and it is important that you actively use as many of them as possible.

The Internet

The Internet can be used in many ways during your job search. Almost every company now posts its openings on job-listing web sites (see Figure 9 for a list of popular sites). This is a useful tool to start your job search with. The Internet can be used in several other ways as well. Many companies post job listings on their company web sites. These postings are often listed under "Careers" or in the "Company Information" section of the web site. You can also find valuable information such as who to contact at human resources or what recruitment practices a company uses. In addition, you can find out more about the company's background and profile.

A less common way that the Internet can help students find jobs is by joining industry-specific message boards. There are thousands of these groups covering every industry or topic you can think of and they can be a valuable networking tool. It is also useful to search for industry associations' web sites. They often provide lists of the companies that are members and this can lead to smaller companies that you do not know of.

Newspapers, Magazines, and Other Publications

Although you may argue that with the use of online job boards, classified ads in newspapers are obsolete, you should still check them. Most companies still use classified ads when posting job openings, and you never know what you may miss in your online searches. You should not limit yourself to reading the classified ads in newspapers that are directly relevant to you. Learn to read between the lines. For example, if there is a notice in the newspaper that an executive in your industry is leaving his firm to start his own company, this presents you with two opportunities. The executive in question will probably be looking to hire. He is probably taking some of his old firm's employees with him, creating openings in that firm as well. Although neither the firm nor the executive has posted openings, you should send them your resumé. By doing this, you will be one step ahead of your fellow job hunters.

Newspapers, magazines, and industry publications can also provide you with information and trends in the industry you are interested in. The business section of newspapers, business magazines (such as *Canadian Business* or *Maclean's*), and industry-specific magazines or publications usually have sections where companies list announcements, tenders, and appointments. This is a good tool to learn about the companies in your industry that may have potential openings. Magazines are also an excellent tool if you are looking for work internationally. By using the same tactics you would with national publications, international publications (such as the *Economist*, the *New York Times*, and *Forbes*) can be used to gather information about potential companies you can apply to.

Unsolicited Applications

Don't be afraid to send your resumé to a company you are interested in working for even if there are no current openings. Make sure you include a polished cover letter (information on this to follow) and follow up with a phone call. Remember to always check their web site first for employment procedures because the company may have particular requirements or an online application.

On-Campus Recruitment and Career Fairs

Starting in September of the year you are graduating, many companies will be coming to your campus to recruit. You should try to attend as many of the information sessions the different recruiters hold as you can; they can open your eyes to job opportunities you were not aware of and can be excellent networking tools.

Your college or university will probably hold at least one career fair during the school year. These events can be industry-specific or directed towards all students. Career fairs are usually held in large public spaces near your campus and consist of several companies' recruiters setting up kiosks in order to provide information about careers at their companies and to recruit students for employment in the following year.

Career fairs can also be very useful if you attend them well prepared. Before attending, try to get the list of companies registered and determine which ones interest you. Research these companies so that when you approach the recruiters you will have relevant questions to ask them that will provide you with a more in-depth picture of the company and more detail about their recruitment process. Employers like students who have a basic knowledge about their company and the industry it is in. You should ask them questions about their corporate culture and what characteristics they value in their employees.

Before the career fair, you should be ready to answer questions about yourself and should have a resumé prepared to give them. You should also have an elevator speech prepared. An elevator speech is a thirty-second commercial for yourself that lets someone know why they should hire you. In the speech, you should focus on the combination of skills, knowledge, and experiences that make you unique. It should be concise, carefully planned, and well practiced. The speech should be phrased in a way that tells the recruiter how you would benefit their company. It should also have a twist that makes you memorable. Make sure that you practice this speech until you sound confident and natural. It should not sound rehearsed or memorized. Remember, a first impression goes a long way and your elevator speech can affect how a recruiter sees you.

At the career fair, you should indicate to the companies that you speak with that you are interested in working for them and that you have done your research. Do not sound overly enthusiastic or you will not sound sincere. Only ask relevant questions and answer questions clearly and concisely. It is important that you do not monopolize the recruiters' time. They are there to meet with all the students present, not just you, and you will leave a bad impression if you don't let them do so. You should dress neatly and professionally, and you should be polite, friendly, and interested in what the recruiters have to say. You should also make sure that you collect company information and business cards so that later you can follow up on the companies that impressed you.

Internships and Volunteering

An excellent way to find job opportunities is through an internship. Not only does it provide practical experience in your field of interest but also excellent networking opportunities. A lot of companies offer internships as a way to start training college or university students that have potential and to form relationships with them. These relationships can develop into offers for permanent employment upon graduation or can lead to other employment opportunities. Volunteering is another useful way to build your skills and gain experience. It can give you insight into different jobs and helps you to get your foot in the door. If you do a good job, the organization may offer you a paid position or refer you to another organization. If you are interested in internships or volunteering, a useful web site is Career Edge (www.careeredge.org). It is a privately financed program that has placed over four thousand interns in Canadian companies. Eighty-five percent of these students have found permanent work in their chosen fields.

Recruiters

You can always use a recruiter or headhunter to help you find a job. A recruiter is used by companies to find well-suited individuals to fill certain positions at their company. They often specialize in certain industries so it is important to ensure you are contacting the right type of recruiter for the field that you are interested in. Some recruiters require a fee for their services. Make sure that you have researched the recruiter thoroughly and that they are both legitimate and suit your needs before giving any money upfront.

Networking

What is networking and how can this assist you in finding your first full-time job? Here, we aren't referring to the networking between computers and their systems but people networking with other people. According to Donna Fisher and Sandy Vilas in their book *Power Networking*, networking is "the process of gathering, collecting, and distributing information for the mutual benefit of you and the people in your network." Keeping this definition in mind, there are numerous things that networking is not. For example, contrary to popular belief, networking is not you just selling yourself or your qualifications or the use of people for your own personal gain. It also does not involve you coercing or manipulating people to do what you want. As stated earlier, networking involves mutual benefit.

Now that we understand what networking is, the question remains: why do people network? An ancient proverb states, "If you want to be prosperous for a year, grow grain. If you want to be prosperous for ten years, grow trees. If you want to be prosperous for a lifetime, grow people." In the search for a job, networking can be the most cost-effective tool when used appropriately. Networking can cost close to nothing, but a referral as a result of networking generates 80% more results than cold calls and approximately 70% of all jobs are found through networking.

Before you begin networking, there are a number of factors that can act as roadblocks to your networking success. As such, it is important to mention them so that you do not fall victim to them throughout the process. The first threat is that of becoming a networking mongrel. A networking mongrel is a person who networks relentlessly and solely for their advancement without concern for the other parties involved. Such a tactic may work for a short time; it is easily detected, however, and causes a lack of trust towards, if not ostracizes, the individual.

Another barrier to networking success is the lone-ranger mentality. People with this mentality believe that if you want something done right, you should do it yourself. Granted, this approach may work in certain situations, but the lone ranger applies this to life in general, feeling that they do not need the help of anyone in order to succeed. If you feel that this is the case, just ask your friends and colleagues how they have acquired their jobs. Undoubtedly, many have acquired their current jobs through someone they knew.

A third barrier that you may encounter is the act of keeping score. In networking, it is believed that if you scratch a person's back they'll scratch yours. Yet, it should not be a tit-for-tat scenario in which you will only perform a favour if guaranteed something in return. You need to have faith that the favour will return some-day, but maybe not today.

Lastly, everyone has fears of rejection or looking needy, which have stopped some individuals from networking at all. These fears are quite common but we recommend that you try your best to over-come these and view networking as conversations between friends. Networking is a common practice and many people partake in it, so by no means should you feel that you will stick out in any way.

How to Network

Having looked at the various factors that can act as barriers in networking, we can move on to learning how to network. According to *Power Networking*, there are six steps in the networking process. The steps are: brainstorming for contacts, knowing your-self, joining groups, presenting yourself well, following up, and staying organized. We will go through each of these one-by-one to give you a clear understanding of what needs to be done in each.

Brainstorming for contacts is the very first step in successful net-working. In the brainstorming sessions, you want to go through the various organizations and groups that you are or have been involved in and list the people you have built relationships with. There are numerous ways of mapping out your contacts. One pop-ular method is the network diagram in which every organization or group is assigned a node, and the individuals, along with their con-tact information, branch off each appropriate node.

The next step is knowing yourself. This may seem very simple, but you would be surprised to see how much work can go into it (see previous section and Figure 1 for more detail). In knowing yourself, we are not asking that you know your favourite colour or your family history; instead, we ask that you be in touch with your true values in life. Take some time to reflect on what is important to you and what you want to get out of your future career. It is also critical to know and be able to convey your accomplishments and your short- and long-term goals. In short, this step asks you to be in touch with yourself and your priorities.

If, while you are getting to know yourself better, you realize that you have not been particularly involved in any organization (or even if you have been), it is good to consider joining additional ones. After all, in networking, it is not just whom you know but also who knows you. What better way to get to know people than by joining a group? We recommend that you try to become a member of a professional organization within your field. An example of this would be the North American Accounting Society. Another option would be to serve on a committee or the board of an organization. And, if you are interested in keeping up with industry trends while meeting new people, you should also look into attending various seminars and courses offered at local venues.

The next step will finally engage you in what you've been waiting to do for this entire section: the actual act of networking. When meeting a person for the first time, it is important that you present yourself properly. The first step is dressing the part. Different events have different dress requirements so be sure to do a bit of research in advance and dress appropriately. You should also prepare yourself by having a memorable self-introduction. (You could prepare one that is similar to the thirty-second elevator speech reviewed earlier.)

By this we mean one that is short, sweet, and relatable. When you are introduced to someone, be sure to listen when they are introduced and focus on what they have to say. The more genuine you are to them, the more genuine they will be in return. During your conversation, use their name a few times to help you remember it.

Networking, however, does not end after a single meet-and-greet but is a continuous process. After meeting a person at a conference or seminar, you should provide them with a follow-up phone call, letter, or e-mail. Now that you have new contacts you want to keep in touch with them, so send them a message once in a while. Keep these messages short, simple, memorable, and easy to respond to. The key is to not wait too long before you send them out, but you also do not want to barrage your contacts. This is where organization will be important.

There are many ways to organize your contacts. In the past, people have used address books or a Rolodex, but with the modern advances in technology, new opportunities have become available. One common method of organizing contact information is through the use of spreadsheets. Such spreadsheets can hold large amounts of information and have the capabilities of sorting through the entries based on the data you need. Make sure your spreadsheet has enough room for pertinent information. Categories most commonly used in these spreadsheets include: names, addresses, phone numbers, companies, job titles, how/where you met them, and interesting notes about them. There are many contact-management software programs that can assist in tracking and communicating with your address books. Some of the more popular ones are: Maximizer, Act, Microsoft Outlook, and Lotus Organizer. Once you have organized your data, you need to be sure to keep up to date with your contacts. Send them an e-mail occasionally and set up a time to get together. One point worth stressing here is that you should try to set a concrete date and time to meet and not just send an e-mail saying, "We should get together sometime." As we all know, attempts such as that rarely materialize into an actual meeting. Another advantage to using the contact-management software includes available features such as calendars for appointments and address books for contact info. Once you schedule a call or appointment, the software will alert you in advance. You can also transfer this information into a Palm Pilot or a Blackberry device.

Networking is a great tool for assisting you in making contacts and this can lead to job opportunities, but it's not the only way to succeed in this competitive environment of job hunting upon graduation from post-secondary education. The resumé, covering letter, job interview, and post-interview process are other extremely important aspects of getting your first full-time job.

Resumé Writing

Creating a resumé is a critical first step in the search for a job. Your resumé is your personal advertisement. It summarizes pertinent facts, awards, and accomplishments that set you apart from the rest of the candidates. Unfortunately, a potential future employer will spend only about forty-five seconds scanning your resumé, so you need to *make those seconds count*! Below, you will find a variety of tips and guidelines that will help your resumé stand out from the others.

Types of Resumés

In general, there are three different types of resumés: chronological, functional, and combination. In a chronological resumé, an applicant lists their work experiences in reverse chronological order, meaning that the most recent experience is at the top of the resumé. This type of resumé works well for people with lots of experience in the field. It highlights what jobs you have had and your progression through your chosen field (see Figure 2). But if you, like many college students, have not had lots of exposure to the workplace, then the functional resumé may be a better choice. A functional resumé brings attention to the candidate's knowledge, skills, and abilities versus past work experience. It is still in reverse chronological order; however, you may introduce new headings to emphasize the skills you bring to the job such as leadership skills, teamwork skills, etc. (See Figure 3). Lastly, there is the combination resumé style that takes the best qualities from both the chronological and functional resumés and puts them into one. Consequently, it emphasizes the candidate's skills while including their job history. Most students graduating from college or university find this resumé style useful as it highlights not only what they have accomplished but also what they can bring to the job. Keeping this in mind, you should review your job experiences and accomplishments and pick the resumé style that works best for you.

Resumé Content

What is included in a resumé tends to vary from person to person and is based on what they can bring to a specific job. However, there are seven key sections that are common among most resumés. These include: personal information, objective, education, work experience, activities, skills, and affiliations. Let's examine each of these one by one.

Your personal information is listed at the top of your resumé. It should include your full and proper name and contact information. If you have a permanent and temporary address, be sure to include both so that the employer knows of all the potential areas you may be able to work. You should also include a home phone number and a cellphone number thus making it easier for the employer to contact you. Be sure to check that whichever phone numbers you list on your resumé have an answering service or voice mail and that the greeting is a neutral one. Lastly, you should include your e-mail address. This e-mail address should be one that sounds professional. Most people tend to use a combination of their first and last name. After all, having a potential employer laugh at your e-mail address may not necessarily be a good thing.

Your personal information is typically followed by an objective. Interestingly enough, employers' number-one complaint is the lack of a specific objective. So here are some tips on how to create one. An objective should:

- Be clear and concise;
- Include the type, if not specific name, of position you are seeking;
- Include your relevant skills; and
- Be tailored to each job.

An example of an ambiguous objective is: "To attain a position with a progressive organization that will fully utilize my talents and skills." As you can see, it lacks each of the points mentioned above and thus lacks the specificity that employers are looking for. A better objective would read: "To attain a position in the field of human resource management that utilizes my organizational and leadership skills." This objective illuminates the type of position the candidate is looking for and highlights the skills and abilities that they can bring to the job.

Most graduating students then follow the objective with a section concerning their education. If you have attained a degree beyond a bachelor or associate's degree, these should again be listed in reverse chronological order. An education section may look as follows:

University of Alberta; Edmonton, Alberta   May 2005
  • BS in Business Administration
  • Major in Management
  • Minor in International Business
  • Dean's List   2003-2004
  • Major GPA – 3.5/4.0

Each entry should begin with the name of the institution and its location. Below this, list your degree and when you plan to graduate. Feel free to also include your majors, minors, and concentrations so that the employer has a better understanding of your specialization. If your cumulative grade-point average (GPA) is greater than 3.0 (out of a 4.0 system) then be sure to list it. If not, list your cumulative GPA for your major if it is higher than 3.0. However, if your GPA does not fulfill these previous criteria, use your discretion when including it in your resumé. Beyond this, you should also be sure to list any honours or awards you have received along with any experiences studying abroad (again in reverse chronological order). In addition, if a position requires the completion of certain types of course work, be sure to list any relevant courses that you may have taken.

In the following section, you should include any work experience you have had. These experiences should again be in reverse chronological order. It is important to be descriptive in your experience—do not simply list the job titles. Remember, a potential employer does not know everything about every job, so be sure to describe your job in detail and highlight your accomplishments. An experience section may look as follows:

Marketing Representative
  Advest Inc.; Edmonton, Alberta   Summer 2000
  • Initiated new direct mail campaign to Western Canada
  • Developed 15 new accounts in a one-year period.
  • Improved phone response times by 10% in my region.

As you can see, the experience entry should include the title of the position, the name of the organization, its location, and the timeframe that you worked there. When describing your experience, be sure to start by using active, power verbs (see Figure 4). You should also try to include experience that applies to the job you are looking to attain. Keeping this in mind, try to include numbers and industry buzzwords if possible. Lastly, be sure not to exaggerate your work experiences. Not only does the interviewer have the ability to contact your former employer but you can also be sure that they will ask very specific questions about your past employment during an interview.

Throughout your years at college or university, you may have been involved in various extracurricular activities. If so, you should include an activities section on your resumé. When listing the activities, your entry will look a lot like the one for your work experience. Be sure to include the name of the organization, the timeframe in which you were involved, any positions held, and specific projects undertaken. The purpose of listing such activities is to show how your past experiences in these organizations, clubs or associations have given you knowledge, skills, or abilities that you can contribute to the company you are applying to.

Most job descriptions list specific skills required in order to successfully perform the tasks expected of the position. As a result, you may wish to list unique skills that both apply to the position and differentiate you from other applicants. Feel free to include the languages you speak and your level of proficiency in each. Certain positions may also ask for the ability to use specific types of software, so list any experience you have had with those. Also, make mention of any other hard and soft skills that you have attained from your previous experiences.

If space permits, you can also include any groups that you are affiliated with. This can include a fraternity or sorority along with any professional organizations in your field such as the Society for Industrial/Organizational Psychology. If you have many affiliations, be sure to include ones that highlight your accomplishments and ones where your experiences are applicable to the field you are pursuing.

Having gone through the many sections of a resumé and what you should strive to include, there are also things that you should not include in a resumé. Unless asked specifically, photos should not be submitted with your resumé along with any information that pertains to your race, gender, marital status, children, or religion. Again, be sure to avoid false or exaggerated information as employers will be sure to verify your qualifications.

Resumé Formatting

Resumés come in all shapes and sizes, and the format you use will depend on the field you are entering. For example, marketing students are encouraged to be creative and to use unique and distinguishing features on their resumés. However, if you wish to play it safe, below is a list of standard practices followed by most in the formatting of their resumé.

- Use white or off-white paper.
- Use standard 8.5 x 11–inch paper.
- Margins should be no less than 0.75 inches and no more than 1.5 inches on all four borders.
- Make your resumé concise and easy to read. It is recommended that recent graduates submit resumés that are only one to two pages long.
- Be consistent in displaying techniques and punctuation.
- The font size should be between 10 to 12 points (12 point is easier to read).
- Use only one or two different types of fonts, preferably Times New Roman or Arial.
- Proofread, proofread, and proofread!

The Cover Letter

When applying for a specific job, most companies will ask you to submit a cover letter along with your resumé. It takes a bit of extra effort to create a good cover letter but it also gives you a great opportunity to convey extra information about yourself to your potential employer. Not only does a cover letter show your potential employers how well you are able to communicate with others but it also provides them with little clues to your personality including your level of professionalism.

Unfortunately, a cover letter is not something you can sit down and write in ten minutes. It takes a bit of preparation and fore-thought. Keeping that in mind, there are five things that we rec-ommend you think about before actually writing the cover letter:

- Your objectives. Are you looking for a full-time/part-time job? An internship?
- Why do you want to work there? Is it the company's rep-utation, products, philosophy, or goals?
- Your knowledge and skills. What are major qualities you have acquired through your experiences?
- The employer's needs. What skills and abilities is the employer looking for?
- Match your skills to the needs of the job and the organi-zation.

Take a moment to jot down your responses to these questions. Now you are ready to begin writing your cover letter. A cover let-ter consists of four parts: the opening, the sales pitch, the flattery, and the request for further action. We'll go through each of these individually.

The opening is an opportunity for you to introduce yourself to your potential employer. It should include your year of study, the name of the school you are attending, and your course of study. A potential opening line may be: "I am a senior at York University graduating in May with a major in electrical engineering." Beyond this, you should also let the employer know exactly why you are writing to them. Try to mention the specific position you are applying for and how you heard about the organization. For example: "I saw your listing for a human resources intern at the McGill University Management Career Centre."

The next section of the cover letter is the sales pitch; this is where you convince the company of why they should select you for the position. Start with an overview of your qualifications as stated in your resumé and then get specific with examples. Be careful not to be too wordy. Here, you can use either paragraph form or bullet points depending on your personal preference.

Having taken the time to express your qualifications for the job, now comes the part of the cover letter dedicated to the company. This part can be considered the "why them" section of the letter. You should take a moment to flatter the reader by stating something positive about the company (i.e. its reputation, sales record, size, social responsibility, etc.). Prospective employers want to know why you have chosen them. However, this section needs to be accompanied with a note of caution. You need to be careful not to be too flattering and thus be perceived as being insincere.

Now comes the request for further action. In this section, you should thank the reader for their time and also suggest the next step. Propose contacting them in a few weeks either by phone or e-mail. But in the last sentence, be sure to restate your contact information in case they wish to get in touch with you. Keeping all of this in mind, a final section may read as such: "Thank you for taking the time to review my qualifications. I look forward to speaking with you soon via e-mail. However, if you require any additional information, feel free to contact me at..."

Now that you have completed the body of your cover letter, we will conclude with a few tips regarding its layout and formatting. If possible, it should be tailored to a specific person. This information may be available on the company's web site or in some company publications. If you are unable to find sufficient contact information from these sources, you may consider calling the company and kindly asking them to assist you in attaining a contact. Beyond this, a cover letter is a formal business letter. As such, it should include the addresses of both parties in the upper-left quadrant of the paper. If you have your own personal stationery with your address already printed, just add the potential employer's address in the upper-left quadrant. A common mistake is placing a comma after the greeting; since you are seeking to be very professional, it is appropriate to follow the greeting with a colon. Also, there should be no indentations; instead, use an extra space between paragraphs (refer to Figure 5 for a sample cover letter).

Interviewing Skills

The purpose of a resumé is not necessarily to get you a job but instead to get your foot in the door and to allow you the chance to interview. It is the interview that is the single most important step in getting a job. You should look at it as a great opportunity to market and sell your qualifications. Your appearance, quality of your answers, confidence level, and presentation are key areas that the interviewer will review. What makes you different from the other candidates is another key criterion. What is your value proposition? The interview process can be divided into three sections: what should be done before, during, and after and interview. We'll be looking at each of these in depth and providing you with tips on how to make it through the process successfully.

Before the Interview

Contrary to popular belief, much effort should go into preparing for an interview. The process requires you to not only know about the company but also about yourself. As stated previously, much of the information about the company and the position can be found on the Internet. Pay particular attention to the culture of the company. Look at its mission statement, values, and the types of activities it is involved in outside of its business. Also be sure to get a detailed job description of the position you are looking to attain. Review the qualifications they are looking for. Afterward, you should look over your resumé beforehand and review the skills that you are looking to highlight during the interview. If you have not done so already, make sure that you stress the ones most applicable to the job. It is also useful to know who will be conducting the interview. Beyond merely knowing the person's name, note the position they hold and how it is related to the job that you are applying for.

Many interviewers tend to ask for a list of about three references. References are people that you have worked with closely or that have known you for an extended period of time who will vouch for your character and work ethic. Unfortunately, references from family members are typically not allowed. Be sure to establish a valid list of them before the interview and bring a copy of the list containing their contact information.

During the interview, you will be asked if you have any questions about the company or the job you are applying for. Even if you believe that you know the company well, it is good to have a list of questions ready to ask the interviewer. Having a list of questions shows that you have done your research and that you are interested in the job—both of which are positive characteristics (for a sample list of questions, refer to Figure 6).

The last step before actually going to the interview is to practice. Have an adult or, if you can find one, a professional in the field provide a mock interview. Many college and university career centres also offer this service. Whichever avenue you may choose, be sure to go through the process as if it were the real thing and ask for constructive feedback in the end.

Having gone through all these steps, you are now ready to tackle the interview. Be sure to get lots of rest the night before. Before you leave for the interview, be sure to bring with you any notes you may have about the company, your list of questions, your references, and a few extra copies of your resumé.

During the Interview

As was stated before, it is not the resumé but the interview that is critical in helping you get a job. This is why we stress that you prepare beforehand particularly through practicing. The interview itself consists of four main stages: the introduction, the interview questions, the applicant's questions, and the closing. It is extremely important that you make a good impression. This does not just apply to the person who is interviewing you but also to everyone you come across during the interview process (the receptionist, people in the elevator, etc.). Be polite, enthusiastic, and friendly with everyone. At the beginning of the interview, make some small talk. In addition to making you more likeable, it's a good way to break the ice and make the interview more comfortable.

When you are meeting your interviewer for the first time, you want to be sure to make yourself memorable. The introduction is your opportunity to set the tone for the interview, so be professional, speak up, and offer a firm handshake. Saying "hello" and shaking hands can be seen as a mere formality, but it also has the purpose of establishing comfort between you and the interviewer.

Most interviewers begin with the standard but highly dreaded "tell me about yourself" question. Even though you may think that this is a question geared mostly toward your personal life, it actually is not. The employer wants to know who you are and how you can fit into the company. So give them what they want. Your answer should consist of three parts. First, state what type of work you want to do or what specific job you are looking to fill. Afterward, stress any skills or accomplishments that are applicable to the position. And finally, be sure to convey interest and eagerness in the position. No one wants to hire someone that does not look interested in the job.

Many interviewers also use standard behavioural interview questions that delve deeper into your experiences and character. Usually, the interviewer will begin these by asking a very specific question such as: "Tell me about a time when you had to deal with a dissatisfied client" or "Give me an example of a time when you had to go above and beyond the call of duty." As daunting as these questions may seem, there is actually a formula to answering them. The process is commonly referred to as the S.T.A.R. tactic, which stands for *Situation, Task, Actions,* and *Result.* In applying the tactic, you first explain the environment you were in and the situation you faced, then you specify the task you were assigned, followed by the actions you took to remedy it, and the concrete results of these actions. Take time to elaborate on points you believe the interviewer may not be familiar with, such as the reporting system in your former position, but try to keep your answer concise.

Another standard type of question asked in an interview is the credential/experience verification question. As suggested by the title, these questions will be geared toward verifying your qualifications for the position. Rest assured that if you have exaggerated a number or the responsibilities held in a position, the interviewer will likely ask questions to reveal your true contributions (for a list of standard questions faced at an interview refer to Figure 7).

Having answered the questions that the interviewer has posed for you, it is now your opportunity to ask any questions you may have. We recommend that you always have a few questions prepared to ask the interviewer to show that you are interested in the position. But you cannot simply ask any question. You want to show the interviewer that you have done your homework, so a question such as, "What does your company do?" is not sufficient. Instead, you can try asking, "What are the company's plans for future growth?" (More of such questions can be found in Figure 6.)

The last part of the interview is the closing. In the last few minutes, be sure to summarize your qualifications and highlight your interest in the position. Afterward, you should try to arrange a specific date and time for your next contact. You can ask: "When should I expect to hear from you?" If you wish to be more proactive, you can continue with: "Do you mind if I give you a call in a few weeks to see where you are in the hiring process?" Whichever approach you choose, be sure to establish the next time you will be speaking to the interviewer.

After the Interview

Congratulations, you have made it through an interview! However, the process does not stop here. After the interview, it is common practice to send a thank-you note to your interviewer within a day of the interview. In this short letter or e-mail be sure to thank the interviewer for taking the time to meet with you. Take the opportunity to comment on any interesting things you learned about the organization/position during your conversation. Also be sure to reiterate your competencies and the expertise you bring to the job. Lastly, if you forgot to mention something during the interview, be sure to include it in the follow-up letter. The follow-up letter is a formal letter just like your cover letter. Drawing on what was discussed earlier, the follow-up letter should include the addresses of both parties in the top-left quadrant, a colon after the greeting, no indentations, and extra space between the paragraphs.

In order to assist yourself through the entire interview process, you should review all the tasks you should have completed before, during, and after so you don't forget anything (please see Figure 8 for a complete checklist).

Getting your first job after graduating from a post-secondary institution can be quite stressful if you don't plan and prepare properly. From writing a resumé to going through the interview, there are numerous areas that can fail if you don't do your homework. We have covered many of the important aspects of this process and we encourage you to research this area in more detail to find more information in areas that you need assistance. This chapter introduces all the key areas and it's up to you to apply your own personal touch so you achieve your own goals. Happy job hunting!

Chapter Eight
Financial Planning

Financial planning has developed over the last twenty years into a very large, bustling industry with many players involved including banks, trust companies, insurance companies, and investment firms. There are over one hundred thousand financial planners across Canada working with hundreds of organizations offering thousands of investments and insurance products. The financial planner can assist you with your plan or you can do it yourself. It all depends on how much time and money you have and to what extent you need the expertise of others if you don't have the expertise yourself. Planning, as we mentioned throughout this book, is a very important part of being successful. We recommend that you plan your finances just as you planned your steps into post-secondary education. Being prepared and understanding all the options will always make it easier going forward. Another area to consider is insurance. There are many products available in this area, and, as we write this book, there are new and innovative products being delivered to the marketplace. More and more companies are packaging their "living benefits" line of products to meet the needs of an aging society as we live longer and need the means to pay for this longer life. From disability insurance to critical and long-term care insurance you will have many choices to make as you grow older. Make these choices wisely and work with an educated financial planner to assist you in accomplishing your goals and objectives for a worry-free life.

What is a Financial Plan?

A financial plan can be two things at once. It can be a picture of where you are now and, potentially, a road map to where you want to be, showing your life goals and how you might achieve these goals.

Having a financial plan is similar in many ways to having a thorough medical exam—your annual physical. For the plan to be effective, you must lay there—your holdings—and expose to the planner your hopes and dreams for the future.

Consider this: your physician knows your health—your aches and pains. They know about your inoculations, blood pressure, and blood type, and they know the complete history of your personal and family medical background.

Your lawyer knows about your will, house, cottage, or other property you may own. They know what your business agreements are in addition to any and all legal undertakings such as divorces and separations, adoptions, and planned giving.

Your accountant knows about your income taxes. They know what you earn—your salary, what interest you receive, and any bonuses or investments. They know your depreciation values, capital gains, and possible tax loopholes. They prepare your profit and loss statements and your balance sheets. They know if you have holding companies or operating companies. Your accountant knows if you have trusts.

It is rare for these professionals to interact. They only need to know what's in the parameter of their own expertise or discipline. A good trusting relationship with your financial planner, however, provides you with a comprehensive plan based on their awareness of your entire life situation.

The planner must know your state of health and that of your spouse. If one of you is in poor health, that is a critical factor. If both of you are in good health but have a family history of either long life or progressive illness, this also must be taken into consideration. Will your assets have to last ten years of retirement to age seventy-five or twenty-five years to age ninety? While the future is unforeseen, will both partners expect to live beyond eighty-five years of age? It is crucial as to the amount of capital that will be required to fulfill this.

The planner needs to know your legal arrangements. Do your investments correspond with your will? Are the beneficiaries of your retirement savings plan (RSP) and your life insurance congruent to your wishes? Will extra insurance be required for children of a previous marriage or former spouse? Is there any thought of leaving a large bequest? Have you thought of returning to live in another country after retirement (i.e. returning to your home country or just immigrating to United States or Australia)? If you have properties, are they to be sold or kept as the family cottage? How does money get taken out of your business? How does your business get sold? Who will buy it? All these tie together with your plan.

This leads to your accountant. Do you have capital gains or recaptured depreciation? The financial planner needs to know how the accountant has arranged your affairs. And are your taxes up to date? Are there any long-term mortgages being held? Your planner, to use a football scenario, is like a quarterback. They see the entire field. They know your playbook and who else is in the lineup. They know whether it is best to play it safe and punt or to try and get some extra yardage and go long. At the end of the day, your planner is your most important asset in helping you obtain your life goals.

Now let's look at what the road map is. Where do you want to be three years from now? Five years from today? When would you like to retire? What are your three main passions in life? Have you ever sat down and asked yourself these questions? Unless you know where you are going, you will end up somewhere else.

Now that we have a grasp on what is a financial plan, how is one put together? Most planners need a good ninety minutes to two hours of candid conversation about you. Some may use a questionnaire; others have the road map in their head and from experience bobbing-and-weaving, depending on how your information is expressed. (If you mention you have a business partner, this may lead to questions of sale and separation of business matters or how long you have worked together or if there are family connections, etc.) This session should prod and poke all aspects of your financial and personal life. If you are less than candid, then your picture is not complete and your map may not lead you where you wish to go. In addition, like all of life's journeys, it is a good idea to pull out the map again from time to time to see what progress has been made and to check your bearings.

Why Plan?

Former U.S. President Harry Truman once said, "Life's tough, it's not for everyone." If you have read this far into the book, it should be obvious to you that you need to plan. The sad part is most people spend more time planning a birthday party or holiday gathering than they spend on planning their own life. A plan puts things down on paper. It focuses the mind. It allows you to think deeper and to prioritize. It puts things in perspective. Planning is not just about money. We suggest you read Stephen Covey's book *Seven Habits of Highly Effective People*. Find out what is important in your life. Is it family, friends, travel, positions, and money?

There are a number of stages in which to plan:

- Short term: tomorrow, next week, next month, the next ninety days.
- Intermediate term: three to six months, next year, the next two years.
- Long term: three years and beyond.
- Life goals.
- For long-term planning, maybe you should work on a mission statement.

Remember, your planning is on paper, not stone. You can and will change your mind. As we move along life's road, our outlook often changes, our philosophy and priorities may shift. Keep your options open as much as possible. When you set your goals, they should be specific, realistic, and measurable. Wanting to be rich is general and too vague. Knowing that you want a million dollars by the time you are forty is something you can focus on, but be flexible. If you're a little short by forty but by forty-five you do it, it's okay. If you only have $900,000, you are not a failure. Just be flexible and realistic.

Every three to five years, take some time to review your life goals. Are they still valid to you? Planning is a journey. It is important to check one's plans on a regular basis. Just as if you are planting a garden, you wouldn't pull the plant up by the roots each day to take a look at it. But every so often, it should be checked. Create lists and check them at regular intervals.

Do You Need a Financial Planner?

Need is a relative measure. If you are just starting out, you may not need a planner. If your needs are relatively simple and you have the time, then you can manage without one. If your needs are more complicated or your time is limited, then you should take advantage of a planner's services. You may feel that you have sufficient expertise to go it alone, but do you have the necessary time? As long as you feel you can manage your affairs and have the time to do so, then, no, you don't need a financial planner. The expertise is available at any level of asset activity. Do you want to get serious about financial management?

Think of a financial planner as being a facilitator. On one hand, the planner works with you to help plan your financial goals. On the other hand, they also help sift through the myriad of financial choices available to help you achieve your goals.

Most of us simply want to get on with our lives. Most of us could change the oil in our cars but we choose to use the services of a mechanic. Very few of us would attempt to cut our own hair and nobody would do their own brain surgery. The bottom line is that most people don't have the time, the knowledge, the resources, or the inclination to plan their financial matters. A financial planner (like a garage mechanic, a barber, or a surgeon) has a specific purpose: to help us expedite, create, and maintain our lifetime investment goals and objectives without requiring a great deal of our ongoing involvement.

Strength comes from recognizing our weaknesses and delegating those tasks to someone who is more capable of performing them. Most people could (and should) use the services of a financial planner. You should recognize that you couldn't do everything as effectively or efficiently as a specialist. Some organizations including banks encourage you to do your own investing. If you rely solely on yourself, who will be there to hold your hand when things go bump in the night? If investing on your own is so easy, why are there so few millionaires? Remember the ancient question: "If you're so smart, why aren't you rich?"

Twelve Reasons to Use a Financial Planner

1. I want to get serious: I played around but who cares what happens with "play money," right? Most of us wake up slowly. Now it's time to stop playing and accumulate some serious money.
2. I don't have the time: With family obligations, being self-employed, or in a small business, there's so much to do!
3. I don't have the expertise: The information is overwhelming.
4. I need help. I can't do it alone.
5. I've never had to deal with this much money: It was okay when I had only a few thousand invested, or won a small lottery, or received a golden handshake, but now...
6. I'm getting older: I can't afford to start over if I make a mistake and lose my investment. I want to retire and enjoy the fruits of my investment. I don't have the time or the energy that I once had.
7. The rules are always changing: The government is always tinkering with the system. I'm finding that I can't keep up.
8. I want to simplify things: I want to concentrate on the things that *I* want to do and keep the rest of my life as simple as possible.
9. My financial institution treats me like a number and my broker just wants to trade: I feel like I'm just one more person at the counter who doesn't really count.
10. I think I know what I want to do but I want somebody to hold my hand.
11. I want to invest, not just save: It's one thing to save for a car or a vacation, but I want to invest for the long term.
12. To help me get where I want to go—financially and in terms of security—faster.

There are several methods for searching out a financial planner. You can look through the yellow pages or check out advertising in various forms of media. One small problem is that anybody can advertise himself as being a financial planner. That's right—anybody. So while an ad will provide a phone number, it doesn't necessarily tell you very much about the financial planner or their firm.

Well, what about attending one of those seminars which are hosted by financial planners? It's nice to actually see a face behind the podium. Someone who is articulate and knowledgeable, but remember that they may not be the person you deal with if you sign up.

You could contact a bank or trust company, but you don't know who they will set you up with and they may not have the credentials you are looking for. Similarly, you could call a mutual fund company for a referral. It will simply give you the name of a financial planner who supports its fund. In either case, the person may be appropriate for your needs but you won't know for sure if you don't shop around.

Probably the most effective approach is to obtain referrals from people you know and trust. Ask friends, relatives, or associates who are in similar financial and social circumstances as your own. Asking a fabulously wealthy uncle may well provide a lead or two but will those leads be able to help his fabulously impoverished niece or nephew?

Once you have some leads, go and interview them personally. Remember that you are not obligated to deal with someone just because you have investigated their services. A recent study revealed that 70% of those looking for a planner found one through referrals. Where did they come from? Of those seeking referrals, 49% found them through friends; 16% through bank managers; 7% through seminars; 6% through lawyers; and 5% through accountants.

Regarding references from bank managers, most of the major banks either own or have some involvement with a brokerage house. While the referral may be a good one, it may not be as objective as it should be. It may simply be company policy to refer a client to one of its own people. To be fair, if your lawyer or accountant provides a referral, ask if they are aligned or have a fiduciary connection with the planner. Again, the advice may be great, but disclosure is good for the soul.

What to Look for in a Financial Planner

Is the planner independent? If they are with a single company, do they have the flexibility to offer a package best suited to your requirements or is he restricted to their company's offerings? Aside from guaranteed investment certificates (GICs), stocks, and bonds, there are over four thousand mutual funds now available. As an independent, your financial planner can access about 90% of them. A single company planner can provide good service but he may not be able to offer as broad a range of products. Ask the planner what products they can offer and what limitations they have.

How long has the planner been in business? There is no absolute requirement on this score. Length of time in business is no guarantee of quality. A planner who has been in the business for many years with a base of only high-end clients may not be the best choice for a smaller investor. Somebody with all the "know how," but less experience, may well compensate by being more attuned to the needs of smaller accounts and will be able to spend more time with their clients. A strong business background or education may compensate well for relatively few years of direct financial-planning experience. The bottom line is that the prospective client will want to see qualifications that engender confidence in the planner's expertise.

What are the planner's credentials? Look at the planner's formal education and their business links within the industry. Is the planner continually upgrading his qualifications and staying current with new services and products?

Can the planner provide references from clients? This is a delicate issue and also involves privacy. In some instances, this may be available.

How is the planner compensated? You definitely want to get this piece of information in the very first interview. Ask about fees charged and commissions earned.

Last, but not least, there is that indefinable factor of "chemistry." Can you relate to this person? Is the planner's attitude toward your financial requirements and goals in tune with yours? Are you confident the planner will protect your privacy and the confidential nature of your finances? Does the planner have an involvement with the community similar to your own?

There are some potential pitfalls to keep in mind. Don't be mesmerized by glamour. A planner may stay in touch by sending cards, calendars, and other items for your birthday and holidays. This may well be a genuine expression on their part. Regardless, as the client, it is up to you to decide whether such "extras" represent what you are looking for in a financial planner. Remember, you're buying the advice, not the glitzy showroom.

Is the planner providing a plan for your financial future or just making a sale? Ask yourself, "Is the planner interested in knowing my entire situation or just about my money?"

What Should a Financial Planner Be Looking for in You?

Once an atmosphere of mutual trust has been established, the planner has to have the total picture of your situation. If there is something you won't or can't divulge, the planner should know why. The planner cannot work effectively seeing only the tip of the iceberg. As in any relationship, trust has to be a two-way street.

The planner must know what you expect in service and must be willing and able to deliver it. Some clients rarely meet with their planners, if at all; others are on the phone every week. How often will your financial planner be reporting to you? How often do you want to talk with your financial planner?

How old is the financial planner relative to you? If the planner is twenty years older than you, then a long-term business relationship is feasible. If the gap is closer to fifty years, you need to know how much longer that planner intends to stay in business and what this means to you in terms of continuity of service. Even if a planner is looking at retirement in a few years, they may still be the best choice for a client given the level of expertise and experience. Remember that you're not married to your planner.

What is the Minimum I Should Look for in a Financial Planner?

A lot depends on your assets. Your decision will be influenced by whether you have, say, $10,000, $100,000, or $500,000 to deal with. If the lower amount represents your entire life's savings, dealing with a single company planner may be right for you. If the larger amount represents the portion of your total assets that you wish to invest, the planner's ability to access the widest possible range of products will likely become more crucial for you. Here's a checklist for both you and your prospective financial planner. These items should be discussed during your first meeting. If the planner doesn't raise them first, *ask*! Here is some useful information to find out:

- The planner's credentials, education, designations, association membership(s), and licence(s).
- The planner's experience. How long have they been in the business? If the planner is new to financial planning, what did they do before? How long does the planner intend to be in business? Are they older and looking at retirement shortly? If so, what continuity can they provide in service?
- How will the planner be compensated?
- Does the planner have errors and omissions insurance?
- Can the planner provide references? Although this is a delicate area (a planner must respect the confidential nature of their relationship with existing clients), do ask.
- What level of support can the planner offer? Are they running a one-person shop or do they have backup? Bear in mind that, while it's nice to talk directly with your planner, their assistant/support staff can probably be just as helpful, or maybe even more so, on routine matters.
- What is the planner's investment philosophy? How does the planner determine the suitability of investments for the client?

You should be prepared to answer the planner's questions:

- Why are you here? What do you want the planner to do for you?
- What is your overall situation—personal, family, health, financial?

- How long are you planning to invest your money?
- What are your current investments?
- When do you see yourself retiring?
- If married, does your spouse's investment plan dovetail with your own?

You will have to put all of your cards on the table once an atmosphere of trust has been established if you want the financial planner to effectively act on your behalf. This isn't a case of the planner being nosy; they really can't help you to prepare and implement an investment strategy if they don't have a good idea of your overall game plan.

As a client, you should have a realistic expectation of what level of service the planner will be providing. If the planner is operating on a commission basis, they will receive more for large investments than smaller ones. Small investors are important, but the simple fact is that the planner can afford to spend less time with them because the return will be less than on larger investors. This doesn't mean a small investor shouldn't expect less than courteous top-quality service. It does mean that someone with a small portfolio shouldn't expect hour after hour of a planner's time.

Is the planner trying to establish a relationship with the client or simply looking to make a sale? Is the client looking for a relationship or simply making an investment? Unless the client initiates it, the planner shouldn't be trying to sell a particular product during the first meeting. You should consider whether you wish to discuss the actual product at this time.

Like any other relationship, trust is a key factor. If you don't feel you can trust the planner after your first meeting, keep looking! Don't be rushed into choosing a planner any more than you would for a doctor, dentist, lawyer, or mechanic. If you are not happy with your first choice of planner at an institution, check with the branch manager or try another branch. If you are dealing with an independent planner and the vibes are not right, go back to your original source if possible.

Does the planner criticize your existing investments? If so, are they really criticizing you or are they following a hidden agenda or pushing "today's special" investment? It's one thing if they review your situation and recommend alternate investments more in keeping with your philosophy and requirements; it's something else if they openly disparage your situation. Parties in good trusting relationships deal from mutual respect, not contempt.

Looking at the Confidentiality Factor

A client should understand the nature of their relationship with a financial planner. If they have an effective relationship, it is likely that the planner will know more about the client than any other professional—your doctor will know about your health but not your finances; your accountant will know about your taxes and your business situation but not your health; your lawyer may be conversant with your will but not your taxes, and so on. Only the planner will have an overview of all aspects of your situation. Only they will know "everything" about you. As we said earlier on, this isn't a case of being nosy; it's what the planner needs to know to get the job done. A planner must be especially careful to respect the confidential nature of this knowledge. By the same token, a client should be aware that a planner does not enjoy the same degree of legal protection as does a priest, lawyer, or doctor regarding their communication with a client.

Are You Married to Your Planner?

No, you aren't married. Still, if your planner moves from their current institution, should you go with them? It depends on whether you have a better relationship with the planner or the institution. Bear in mind that it may cost you to move your investment and you should investigate this factor before making a decision. Is the cost worth the move? If you stick with your planner, one option may be to invest new money with them and, in order to avoid penalties, wait until your current investments mature before switching them over.

The Bottom Line Is Trust!

In a recent survey, 60% of respondents said that trust was the most important aspect they looked for in a financial planner. Only 31% cited performance and 9% looked at processing and procedure.

Education—to a Degree

There really wasn't a financial-planning industry prior to 1990. Financial activity was divided between the traditional four pillars of the investment community: banks, trust companies, stock brokers, and insurance companies. Financial planners were usually bank managers, trust officers, stock brokers, and insurance agents.

As the industry grew and matured and as government and tax legislation made life less than simple, the need for specialized education became important. Over the years, designations have become more sophisticated and include:

- Chartered Life Underwriter (CLU)—The CLU involves three years of education and examinations on subjects including taxation, pension plans, group benefits, estate planning, accounting, and life insurance law.
- Chartered Financial Consultant (ChFC)—Since 1989 in Canada. Following completion of the CLU, the ChFC requires a further three years of education in comprehensive financial planning including studies in risk management, family law and advanced wealth accumulation planning. This designation was retired in 1999 to give prominence to the Certified Financial Planner. Both the CLU and the ChFC are offered by Advocis.
- Registered Financial Planner (RFP)—A comprehensive six-hour examination on all areas of financial planning for those who have been active in financial planning for at least two years. This designation was highly coveted by top financial planners until 2002 when it was retired in favour of the CFP.
- Certified Financial Planner (CFP)—Three years of study and examinations cover such planning aspects as investment strategies, financial markets, and taxation, offered by the Financial Planners Standards Council of Canada. This designation is being promoted as the standard financial planning designation in Canada, the United States, and throughout the world.
- Fellow of the Canadian Securities Institute (FCSI)—This

designation is offered by the Canadian Securities Institute and is primarily conferred to licensed security representatives (stockbrokers). This designation involves many years of study and experience in wide areas of investment, risk management, and financial planning.

All designations have requirements for minimum levels of continuing education. A financial planner may belong to one or more of the following associations: Advocis (a recent merger of the Canadian Association of Financial Planners and the Canadian Association of Insurance and Financial Advisors), the Investment Funds Institute of Canada (IFIC), the Independent Life Insurance Brokers of Canada, and the Canadian Institute of Financial Planners.

What value do such memberships confer? The associations offer both resources and an avenue for continuing education. Each association imposes standards of conduct and permits a financial planner to be held accountable to a code of ethics as established by their peers. Education and designations obtained outside of the financial planning field may also indicate related ability. These include Certified General Accountant (CGA), Registered Investment Advisor (RIA), Chartered Accountant (CA), Bachelor of Laws (LLB), or Master of Business Administration (MBA).

That being said, formal training does not, by itself, necessarily confer competence. Many financial planners have gained immense knowledge through "self-learning" with little formal training. A hands-on experience is also a factor to consider when evaluating a financial planner. Relevant education and designation(s) are important, but, remember, you must also have a good relationship with your financial planner before you can place your confidence in them.

How Does Your Financial Planner Make Money?

Commission is not a four-letter word! Unfortunately, commission is a dirty word to many people. There is a perception that someone who receives a sales commission is more interested in the commission than the best interest of the client. However, not all persons on commission "peddle," "hawk," or "push" products. While there will always be salespeople who take advantage of commissioned sales, the vast majority is comprised of responsible professionals who have the client's best interest in mind. A commission shouldn't be a barrier to receiving quality service! It's not the commission or fee that you pay (or don't pay) but, rather, the professional advice you get (or don't get) which determines your ultimate investment performance.

The great majority of financial planners operate on a commission basis. Perhaps 80% to 85% of planners receive their compensation in this manner. A client goes to a planner who helps him develop a financial plan and then implements it. The planner's time and expertise are paid for by the commission derived from the implementation process.

Commissions on mutual funds and segregated funds can take various forms: front-end load, back-end load, or deferred sales charges in addition to finder fees and trailer or service fees.

Front-end commissions on the purchase of mutual funds are paid when a transaction takes place. They are usually in the 2% to 5% range but can go as high as 9%. In addition, stock-brokerage firms charge a commission on each purchase and sale of stocks and bonds.

Back-end or deferred fees are triggered as a redemption fee when an investor sells their investment. The advantage of this sort of fee is that all of your money is put into your investment initially. You pay no direct commission if you invest for up to seven years. The planner is paid by the fund company. While you can switch from your investment to another fund within the same mutual-fund company, should you wish to move to another company, there could be a charge of up to 5% to do so.

Finder fees are paid by trust companies, insurance companies, and other financial institutions for placement of GIC-type investments. This fee is paid from the difference between the guaranteed interest rate paid to you and what is actually earned by the financial institution on your investment.

"Trailers" or service fees are often paid by institutions to financial planners, brokers, and sales representatives on an annual basis as compensation for ongoing services provided to the client. This fee usually ranges between 0.25% to 1.0%. Trailers are derived from the management fee charged by the institution and are not a separate charge to the client.

Fee-for-service is the second most popular means of compensating a planner for his work. Fee-for-service is used by, perhaps, 10% to 12% of financial planners. Under this approach, the client pays the planner on an hourly rate to develop a plan. The fee ranges from $50 to $200 per hour. There is no commission and the planner is not involved in the implementation phase once they have developed and presented the financial plan. Fees can take different formats besides the hourly rate as some planners may charge a flat fee for services rendered.

There is a hybrid combining commission sales and fee-for-service whereby the planner will charge a fee for developing the plan and then offset the fee against the commission if they implement the plan as well.

The planner probably doesn't get all of the commissions and service fees; some of it "sticks to the pipes." A great deal of the commission may be directed to the planner's brokerage or investment house.

Finally, there is the no-load approach. You can deal with a bank, trust company, or discount broker where you can obtain advice over the phone or in person and invest your money through one of their funds. The drawback to this approach is that you may not deal with the same person on an ongoing basis, making a long-term relationship difficult to establish.

How can you get your dry-cleaning without a ticket? The short answer is that you can't. Financial planning is like most everything else in life—you get what you pay for. Most people don't take advantage of fee-for-service planners because they have short arms and deep pockets when it comes to paying for financial planning. When you choose to use a no-load or minimal-fee service, you also dispense with the advice and suggestions of a knowledgeable planner. If you have the time and know-how to devote to your own financial activities, this may be a suitable alternative. However, for the majority of investors, this means that you are trying to play the game without a plan. Guess how many teams get to the championships without a plan?

It's all in how you look at it. Many investors get hung up on the size of the management fee of some mutual funds. How much am I being charged? Instead, investors should be looking at the net results of their investment. How much did I make at the end of the day? By all means, review the fees and consider whether they are justified. Your investment should be justified on the basis of the final result.

Single-Company Planners vs. Independent Planners

A single-company planner is an individual who is aligned with a firm. This means the planner places investments only with the firm that employs them. Even if the financial planner is knowledgeable about the market, they will have a limited selection of investments to offer the client. Although it is possible to reach your financial goals through a single-company planner, you may be limited in your investment options.

The independent financial planner may be able to offer more objective advice because of the large number of options available to them including mutual funds, stocks, bonds, GICs, etc. Although there appears to be an infinite number of choices on the market, the planner will narrow that to a short list of about twenty. For example, there are currently more than four thousand mutual funds. A good independent planner will exercise due diligence in evaluating funds. This means they will sift through the various funds, attend conferences, go to road shows (informational meetings held to discuss current or new mutual funds), and often meet with the fund manager to determine the investment philosophy and management style behind the funds best suited to you.

It should be made clear that some "independent planners" also sell "proprietary products." Proprietary products are either mutual funds or money-management services that are owned by the institution that sponsors the planner. There is nothing wrong with these investments per se as long as there is proper disclosure. Some people have the perception that a financial planner who represents a large corporation with a national or provincial base may be the best choice. However, you should bear in mind that you're ultimately buying the investment advice of the planner, not the institution.

The planner's role is to help you make suitable decisions to realize your financial goals through appropriate selection and continued review. If your investment is handled by a competent planner, there is no advantage in using a national firm over a boutique planner. Should you have a falling-out with an independent planner, you can move your portfolio to another planner. If you are dealing with a single-company planner, your investment is committed within the company and can be moved only at maturity or with a penalty.

Synergy

What other resources can your financial planner offer? Is the planner able to refer the client to a lawyer or accountant? Can the planner draw upon the knowledge of specialists inside their organization? If these specialists are not "in-house," do they have a working relationship with a lawyer experienced in wills and trusts—an accountant, an income-tax preparation service, and agents for various forms of insurance? (The planner may handle insurance needs directly.)

A financial planner does not know everything (perhaps we should have warned you to sit down before breaking this news). The planner shouldn't be afraid to say, "I don't know, but I'll find out for you." Something new is always around the corner. The real issue is: Is the planner ready, willing, and able to find out what you need to know in a timely fashion? "No man is an island," wrote the poet John Donne. Just as we eventually come to the realization that we can't do it alone, we cannot expect the planner to know everything all the time. As a matter of fact, if they think they do, watch out!

A financial planner is a valuable asset for *what* they know but also for *who* they know and *where* they have been. Like a honey bee moving from flower to flower, a planner meets with many clients, attends countless meetings, reads reams of articles, and consults with a parade of related professionals. In a year, the planner may have met with a number of fund managers, listened to a wide variety of investment philosophies and strategies, and even travelled to distant lands to observe first-hand that region's economy and to listen to local officials and business figures. A well-read, well-travelled, knowledgeable planner can make a world of difference to your financial plan and offer you a broad and unique perspective.

You and Your Planner—Common Objectives

How does your planner determine your comfort level? You and your planner must agree on *your* desired level of risk and investment objectives. This level should be established at the beginning of your relationship and it is worth keeping in mind as time passes. Your planner may use a questionnaire such as an "investment policy statement" or "profile" to help establish a client's level of risk acceptance.

If you are looking for a relatively safe and steady investment, you will likely find it an alarming experience to be working with a financial planner who thinks it's inconvenient to use a parachute while skydiving. Your planner should discuss not only your risk acceptance but a classic strategy that dictates you spread your money around (diversify) to minimize the negative effect of a particular investment turning sour. This will become particularly important for clients with portfolios containing, say, $100,000 plus. It is wise to remember that sailing on the investment ocean is never free of upsets or change. A proper diversification strategy can help to smooth out your trip and overcome rough stretches of water.

Beware of a financial planner who acts as a "market timer." For example, if the planner starts recommending that you move in and out of mutual funds as if they were stocks—watch out! Mutual funds are designed for long-term investment. Rapid turnover between funds may improve the planner's commissions but what will the client gain? Is rapid turnover helping the client to meet their financial goals?

Saying Goodbye

Why would you part ways with your financial planner?

- You decide that your financial planner is no longer meeting your needs.
- The planner has changed. Perhaps it's a case of your

asset base being small and, as the planner's practice has grown, you are now "too small" to warrant their attention.

• The planner has changed organizations. But you're more comfortable with the organization than with the planner.

• The quality of service and advice has declined. Perhaps the planner has become lazy or has grown so busy to the point where time and support staff is not adequate to meet your needs.

• The planner is getting on in years and has semi-retired or is no longer willing or able to handle the accounts.

• The planner has not upgraded their skills and knowledge over time. This could mean that you are not being informed about new products or changes in the industry.

• The investment(s) originally proposed by the planner are no longer producing the desired results or, quite frankly, may have turned bad.

• You've changed. Your assets or needs have changed over the years and now you feel the financial planner no longer meets your requirements.

• You (or your planner) have moved and you would be more comfortable dealing with a planner who you can meet with personally as required.

How to Go About Moving

Details on moving depends on what type of investments you have. If the bulk of your portfolio is in nominee for or RRSPs, changing financial planners can usually be done through a simple "change of representative" form or a simple transfer form. If instruments such as stocks, bonds, or mortgages are involved, they don't necessarily have to be sold and reinvested. It is possible to transfer them "in kind," which means the investment is transferred as is. As a client, you should understand that moving assets may cost you money. The financial planner should ensure that you are aware of this, if applicable.

Both parties should realize that they are not married to each other. However, an investor may have "de facto in-laws" when dealing with a single company planner. If the investor changes planners, they must consider that the new planner will be selected from the staff within the company. If the investor changes over to an independent planner, they must choose whether to wait until their investments with the firm mature or to transfer them immediately with a possible penalty. As an investor, you should understand your rights and options. In particular, you are no more obligated to remain with your current investment firm than you are to follow the departing planner. You can stay with one or the other or select someone new. Aside from any penalties that may be applicable for early withdrawal, you have no obligations.

How Not to Say Goodbye

There are some distinct barriers to hurdle for those contemplating the "I'll do it myself!" form of parting. First of all, you will have to use the services of a representative or discount broker to purchase many investments. If you are dealing in mutual funds, the broker will receive trailer or service fees. So you will have to deal with somebody, somewhere, sometime. More important, if you needed a financial planner to get to this stage of the game, why would you not need one now? It comes back to the issues of time and expertise. If a mechanic's time was worth less than our own when it came to changing our oil last month, why should things be different this month? You're not obligated to deal with a particular financial planner any more than you are with a particular mechanic.

Life Insurance—Starting Out

Traditionally, life insurance took care of two concerns. Dying too soon and living too long. Today, with the decline in interest rates and alternative investments, most insurance is bought for protection. It is to insure against loss—the loss of your life. There are two basic benefits: death insurance and living benefits.

Let's start with death insurance, or, as it is sugar coated, life insurance. What is life insurance? It's a cash payment to those you leave behind in the event of your premature death to pay what must be paid or to fulfill your wishes for your family and loved ones. How much is enough? Well, how much do you need? If you are single and have no debt and no dependents, then you will need very little, say, $10,000 to $25,000 to cover your last expenses such as funeral costs and cleaning up any taxes or any outstanding debts. If you are married and have dependents (either children or aging parents), and you own a home with a mortgage, you may need a lot more. A rough rule of thumb is five to ten times your annual salary.

Consider this: A couple, "John" and "Mary," are married. They have a house with a mortgage of $150,000 and two children aged three and five. Both couples work and have a combined income of $80,000. Should either John or Mary die suddenly, could the surviving spouse maintain their current standard of living alone? Probably not. Even if the mortgage was paid off, it would still be a struggle. Aside from the emotional trauma of the loss, there's the financial loss. There are bills to pay, food, clothing, property taxes, income taxes, maintenance, education for the two children, automobile purchases, maintenance, car insurance, etc.

Life insurance provides choices and the freedom to choose. The surviving spouse could elect to take a three to six month sabbatical to spend with the children. If the surviving spouse was originally a stay-at-home parent, that plan could continue. There could also be extra money available that could take care of childcare or nannies, etc. The coverage could take care of elder parents.

The Types of Coverage

First, speak with your parents. Did they buy life insurance for you when you were young? This may contain a valuable option called guaranteed insurability. This will allow you to buy life insurance without medical evidence if your health is less than perfect. If you are asthmatic, diabetic, etc., this is very helpful, but if you're in good health, you can shop around.

Second, check with your employer. Your group coverage will supplement your needs, but a warning, you must be employed to collect. If you lose your job or you are laid off, you lose your insurance. Yes, you could convert your group coverage, but this is very expensive. It is better in the long run to play it safe, buy your own insurance separately, and count on the employers' insurance as a top-up or as extra.

What kind of insurance should you get? If dollars are tight or you have a regular savings program, buy term insurance. We prefer the ten-year renewable term. The coverage and the premium are guaranteed for ten years and can be renewed. If you are in good health at the end of the ten-year period, you can shop around. If not, you can renew without providing medical evidence.

Term insurance is a commodity. As long as the company is financially sound, it doesn't matter; the coverage will be there. The protection will be there. Be sure to compare—not only the current rates but also the renewal rates. A recent survey for a non-smoking male aged thirty for $250,000 of a ten-year renewable term illustrated forty-one companies with a premium range of $185 to $440 annually. Most life-insurance brokers can provide you with such a quotation service.

Aside from covering expenses today such as child education, childcare, mortgages, etc., an eye should be held to the future. Life insurance is also a valuable tool for estate conservation. When the last of the two spouses passes away, all of the RRSP proceeds become fully taxable. This could result in tens of thousands to hundreds of thousands of dollars becoming taxable. Proper life insurance would help pay these bills. It would make the difference between maintaining the family cottage or vacation spot or being forced to sell it to pay capital gains. It would make the difference on the size of the estate that your children or grandchildren will inherit.

You don't have to die to collect. There are a number of living benefits. The first is critical-illness insurance. This is a relatively new form of insurance. In the event that you suffer from certain specific illnesses or diseases such as cancer, heart attack, multiple sclerosis, etc., or a number of other specified ailments, a cash living benefit is paid to you. This is a tax-free lump sum paid out in the event of one of these diseases. You don't have to die to receive this insurance payout.

Another member of the living-benefits insurance group is disability insurance. Disability insurance pays in the event that you're unable to perform your job due to sickness or illness. This disability usually pays a tax-free payment every month during your disability up to and including the age of sixty-five or even beyond. In addition, some companies do allow people who are terminally ill to have an advance on their life insurance prior to death in order that they may take care of some last wishes.

Life insurance, critical-illness insurance, and disability insurance are protection. It protects you and your family from the unknown. The few dollars that it costs are usually and, in most cases, vastly outweighed by the benefit and peace of mind that they bring.

As you decide on the many aspects of investing, saving, choosing a financial planner and insurance products, and how you plan on meeting your financial needs as you grow older, there are many questions you must ask yourself along the way. The best advice we can offer here is that of being informed. Don't be afraid to ask questions and find out the costs and benefits associated with all the decisions you make or don't make. Planning for your future is very important, and having the financial resources to meet your plans is just as crucial. In many cases, you can have a plan, but if you can't afford to pay for the plan, you will not be able to meet your goals in life. You need air in your sails to guide your boat!

Appendix A
Student Loan Web Sites

Alberta
> Students Finance — Alberta Learning Information Service
> http://www.alis.gov.ab.ca/studentsfinance/main.asp

British Columbia
> Student Services Branch
> Advanced Education, Training, and Technology
> http://www.aved.gov.bc.ca/studentservices/

Manitoba
> Student Financial Assistance — Department of Education and
> Training
> http://www.gov.mb.ca/educate/sfa/pages/sfaFrontDoor_en
> .html

New Brunswick
> Student Services Branch — Department of Advanced
> Education and Labour
> http://www.studentaid.gnb.ca/

Newfoundland and Labrador
> Student Aid Division — Department of Education, Thompson
> Student Centre
> http://www.edu.gov.nf.ca/studentaid/

Northwest Territories
> Student Financial Assistance Program — Department of
> Education, Culture and Employment
> http://www.nwtsfa.gov.nt.ca/

Nova Scotia

Student Assistance Office — Department of Education and Culture

http://studentloans.ednet.ns.ca/

Nunavut

Financial Assistance for Nunavut Students — Adult Learning and Post-Secondary Services, Department of Education

http://www.nac.nu.ca/student/fans.htm

Ontario

Student Support Branch — Ministry of Training, Colleges, and Universities

http://osap.gov.on.ca

Prince Edward Island

Student Aid Division, Department of Education

http://www.edu.pe.ca/studentloan/resources/index.asp

Quebec

Student Financial Assistance Programs — Ministère de l'Éducation

http://www.afe.gouv.qc.ca/english/indexAng.asp

Saskatchewan

Student Financial Assistance — Post-Secondary Education and Skills Training

http://www.student-loans.sk.ca/

Yukon

Student Financial Assistance Unit — Department of Education

http://www.education.gov.yk.ca/advanceded/sfa/

Appendix B
Calculating Your Education Expenses

$ Cost

Tuition:

     First Semester _____

     Second Semester _____

Compulsory Fees: _____

Books:

     Course: _____ Textbook:_____

     Course: _____ Textbook:_____

     Course: _____ Textbook:_____

     Course: _____ Textbook:_____

     Course: _____ Textbook:_____

Equipment:

     1._____

     2._____

     3._____

     4._____

     5._____

Child Care Cost:

     Cost per week _____

     # of weeks needed _____

     Total Cost = _____

Transportation:

     Type of Transportation: _____

     Cost of one-way trip: _____

     Cost of one-way + return trip: _____

Personal Expenses (i.e. Medical related): _____

TOTAL ALLOWABLE EDUCATIONAL EXPENSES _____

Appendix C
School Budget

Expense Item	Living at Home	Campus Residence	Single Apartment	Shared Dwelling
Tuition & Fees				
Books				
Transportation				
Accommodation (Rent)				
Food				
Clothing				
Entertainment				
School Supplies				
Computer/ Printer				
Health Insurance				
Insurance (Car; Home)				
Utilities				
Cellphone				
Phone				
Cable				
Internet				
Laundry				
Other				
Total cost	$	$	$	$

Enter the estimated cost associated for each item to see what your cost will be in each situation. The cost for each type of accommodation will vary as well as the various costs associated with the selected dwelling.

Appendix D
Apartment Search Checklist

	1	2	3	4
Location				
Landlord Contact				
Name & Phone				
Rent				
Deposit				
# of Rooms				
# of Bedooms				
# of Bathooms				
Washer/Dryer				
Separate Entrance				
Parking				
Storage				
Yard Space				
Utilities				
Cable				
Internet				
Closet Space				
Sunlight				
Distance to School				
Distance to Groceries				
Distance to Laundry				
Other				

Figure 1
Analyze Your Ideal Work Environment

Do you like to work with data, people, or things?

_____

Why?

_____

_____

_____

_____

_____

How important are salary, benefits, and job stability?

_____

Explain why.

_____

_____

_____

_____

Is it important that you are your own boss?

_____

Why?

_____

_____

_____

_____

Describe your ideal working environment:

_____

_____

_____

_____

Describe your ideal colleague(s):

_____
_____
_____
_____

How important is job stimulation?

_____

Why?

_____
_____
_____
_____

What size company would you like to work for?
Large_____Medium_____Small_____
Why?

_____
_____
_____
_____

7. Do you have a preference as to where you want to work: in a specific city, geographical area, or climate?

_____
_____
_____

If yes, please describe:

_____
_____
_____
_____

8.   Which of the following are important to you and why?
Money? Why/why not:

_____

Power? Why/why not:

_____

Prestige? Why/why not:

_____

Security? Why/why not:

_____

Travel? Why/why not:

_____

Opportunities? Why/why not:

_____

9. Describe the ideal:
Job:_____

_____

_____

_____

Manager:

_____

_____

_____

_____

Coworkers:

_____

_____

_____

_____

Source: Guffey, Mary Ellen, Kathleen Rhodes, and Patricia Rogin. *Business Communication: Process and Product.* **4th Canadian ed. Toronto: Thomson-Nelson, 2005. (521-522)**

Figure 2
Sample Resumé

MICHELLE E. MARTIN
49 South Edgeware Road
St. Thomas, ON N5P 2H5
(519) 555-9322

Objective

To attain a position with a financial-services organization installing accounting software and providing user support, where computer experience and proven communication and interpersonal skills can be used to improve operations.

Experience

Accounting Software Consultant, Financial Specialists, London, Ontario, June 2000 to present

Design and install accounting systems for businesses like 21st Century Real Estate, Illini Insurance, Aurora Lumber Company, and others. Provide ongoing technical support and consultation for regular clients. Help write proposals such as a recent one that won a $250,000 contract.

Office Manager (part-time), Post Premiums, London, Ontario
June 1999 to May 2000

Conceived and implemented an improved order processing and filing system. Managed computerized accounting system; trained new employees to use it. Helped install local-area network.

Bookkeeper (part-time), Sunset Avionics, St. Thomas, Ontario
August 1998 to May 1999

Kept books for small airplane rental and repair service. Performed all bookkeeping functions including quarterly internal audit.

Education
University of Western Ontario, London, Ontario
   Business Administration, June 2000
   Graduated with an A average.

Computer Associates training seminars, summer and fall 2000.
   Certificates of completion.
   Seminars in consulting ethics, marketing, and ACCPAC
   accounting software.

Special Skills
Proficient in WordPerfect, PageMaker, Lotus 1-2-3, and Excel.
Skilled in ACCPAC Plus, MAS90, and Solomon IV accounting soft-
   ware.
Trained in technical writing, including proposals and documenta-
   tion.
Competent at speaking and writing French.

Honours
Dean's List, three semesters.
Member, Academic Affairs Advisory Council, UWO, 1998-2000.

Figure 3
Sample Resumé

DONALD W. VINTON
67 Partridge Crescent
Thompson, MB R8N 1A3
(204) 555-4981

Objective
To attain a position in sales or marketing with opportunities for advancement and travel.

Sales/Marketing Skills
Demonstrated lawn-care equipment in central and western Manitoba.

Achieved product sales amounting to 120% of forecast in competitive field.

Personally generated over $25,000 in telephone subscriptions as a part of President's Task force for the Alumni Foundation.

Conducted telephone survey of selected businesses in two counties to determine potential users of farm equipment and to promote company services.

Successfully served forty or more retail customers daily as clerk in electrical-appliance department of national hardware store.

Communication Skills
Conducted survey, analyzed results, and wrote a twenty-page report regarding the need for developing a recycling program at the University of Manitoba.

Presented talks before selected campus classes and organizations encouraging students to participate in the recycling program.

Announced sports news for CGNF, the college radio station.

Organizational/Management Skills
Helped conceptualize, organize, and conduct highly successful campus campaign to register student voters.

Trained and supervised two counter employees at Pizza Bob's.

Organized my courses, extracurricular activities, and part-time employment to graduate in seven semesters. Graduated with a B+ average.

Education

University of Manitoba, Winnipeg, Manitoba, BBA, 2001

Major: Business Administration with sales and marketing emphasis, A average in major.

Sault College, Sault Ste. Marie, Ontario

Courses in General Studies and Business Administration.

Employment

Pizza Bob's, University of Manitoba, 1999-2001

Bellefonte Manufacturers Representatives, Winnipeg, Summer 1998

Figure 4
Commonly Used Action Verbs

Acted	Convince	Formulated	Planned
Addressed	Counseled	Founded	Prepared
Administered	Created	Generated	Processed
Allocated	Critiqued	Guided	Programmed
Analyzed	Customized	Identified	Projected
Appraised	Demonstrated	Illustrated	Promoted
Approved	Designed	Initiated	Publicized
Arbitrated	Developed	Inspected	Purchased
Arranged	Devised	Instituted	Recorded
Assembled	Diagnosed	Interpreted	Recruited
Assessed	Directed	Interviewed	Referred
Assisted	Drafted	Introduced	Remodeled
Audited	Edited	Invented	Repaired
Balanced	Educated	Investigated	Represented
Budgeted	Engineered	Maintained	Researched
Built	Established	Managed	Revitalized
Calculated	Evaluated	Marketed	Screened
Catalogued	Examined	Monitored	Solved
Clarified	Executed	Motivated	Specified
Classified	Expedited	Negotiated	Summarized
Coached	Explained	Operated	Surveyed
Collaborated	Extracted	Organized	Systematized
Collected	Fabricated	Originated	Tabulated
Compiled	Facilitated	Overhauled	Translated
Computed	Familiarized	Performed	
Conceptualized	Forecasted	Persuaded	

Figure 5
Sample Cover Letter

Donald W. Vinton
634 Tupper Street
Thunder Bay, ON P7A 4A5

May 29, 2005

Mr. Richard M. Jannis
Vice President, Operations
Sports World, Inc.
245 Maitland Street
London, ON N6B 2Y2

Dear Mr. Jannis:

Today's *London Free Press* reports that your organization plans to expand its operations to include national distribution of sporting goods, and it occurs to me that you will be needing highly motivated, self-starting sales representatives and marketing managers. I have these significant qualifications to offer:

- Four years of formal training in business administration, including specialized courses in sales management, retailing, marketing promotion, and consumer behaviour.
- Practical experience in demonstrating and selling consumer products, as well as successful experience in telemarketing.
- Strong interest in most sports and good communication skills (which helped me become a sportscaster at UWO's radio station CGNF).

I would like to talk with you about how I can put these qualifications, and others summarized in the enclosed resumé, to work for Sports World as it develops its national sales force. I'll call during the week of June 5th to discuss your company's expansion plans and the opportunity for an interview.

Sincerely yours,

Donald W. Vinton

Enclosure

Figure 6
Questions to Ask an Interviewer

Why is this position open?

How often has it been filled in the past five years? What were the main reasons?

What would you like done differently by the next person who fills this position?

What are some of the objectives you would like to see accomplished in this job?

What is most pressing? What would you like to have done in the next three months?

What are some of the long-term objectives you would like to see completed?

What are some of the more difficult problems one would have to face in this position?

How do you think these could best be handled?

What type of support does this position receive in terms of people, finances, etc.?

What freedom would I have in determining my own work objectives, deadlines, and methods of measurement?

What advancement opportunities are available for the person who is successful in this position, and within what time frame?

In what ways has this organization been most successful in terms of products and services over the years?

What significant changes do you foresee in the near future?

How is one evaluated in this position?

What accounts for success within the company?

Important: Some questions may or may not be appropriate for your interviewing situation.

Figure 7
Standard Interviewer's Questions

Tell me about yourself.

What do you want to do with your life?

Do you have any actual work experience?

How would you describe your ideal job?

Why did you choose this career?

When did you decide on this career?

What goals do you have in your career?

How do you plan to achieve these goals?

How do you evaluate success?

Describe a situation in which you were successful.

What do you think it takes to be successful in this career?

What accomplishments have given you the most satisfaction in your life?

If you had to live your life over again, what would you change?

Would your rather work with information or with people?

Are you a team player?

What motivates you?

Why should I hire you?

Are you a goal-oriented person?

Tell me about some of your recent goals and what you did to achieve them.

What are your short-term goals?

What is your long-range objective?

What do you see yourself doing five years from now?

Where do you want to be ten years from now?

Do you handle conflict well?

Have you ever had a conflict with a boss or professor? How did you resolve it?

What major problem have you had to deal with recently?

Do you handle pressure well?

Figure 8
Interview Checklist

Before

Review job description and analyze how your background matches it.

Identify your two or three best selling points about your candidacy specific to the job.

Determine how your values would compliment those of the company.

Be ready to answer the top three questions asked.

Learn about the company's financials, its executive leaders, its products, and its competitors.

During

Arrive ten minutes early.

Bring two copies of your resumé.

Be ready to complete a job application.

Avoid saying too little or too much.

Match the tone and energy level of the interviewer.

Ask for clarification of any question you do not fully understand.

Ask at least two of your own questions and know what the next step is after the interview.

Keep eye contact, smile when most appropriate, and always convey enthusiasm about the position.

After

Take notes of the ideas, good points, and bad points that summarize the interview.

Send a thank-you letter or e-mail within a day.

Call within two weeks to find out the status of the hiring process and your next step.

Figure 9
Useful Web Sites

Career-Planning Information and Resources
Canada Career Consortium –
   http://www.careerccc.org/ccc/nav.cfm?l=e
Career Development eManual at the University of Waterloo –
   http://www.cdm.uwaterloo.ca/index.asp
JobFutures – http://jobfutures.ca
The Vault.com – http://www.vault.com
Workopolis – http://www.workopolis.com

Canadian Job-Search Sites
Best Jobs Canada – http://www.bestjobsca.com
Canadian Job Bank – http://jb-ge.hrdc-drhc.gc.ca/Intro_en.asp
Career Edge: Canadian Internship Organization –
   http://www.careeredge.org
JobBoom – http://www.jobboom.com
JobShark.com – http://www.jobshark.ca
Monster – http://www.monster.ca
MonsterTrak (for students) –
   http://www.monstertrak.monster.com
Working – http://working.canada.com
Workopolis – http://www.workopolis.ca
WorkopolisCampus (for students) – http://www.workopolis-
   campus.ca
Yahoo! Canada Hot Jobs – http://ca.hotjobs.yahoo.com

Non-Profit Organization Job-Search Sites
CharityVillage.com – http://www.charityvillage.ca
Green Dream Jobs –
   http://www.sustainablebusiness.com/jobs/index.cfm
Idealist.org – http://www.idealist.org
Volunteer.ca – http://www.volunteer.ca/index-eng.php

Bibliography

Fisher, Donna, and Sandy Vilas. *Power Networking Second Edition : 59 Secrets for Personal & Professional Success.* 2nd ed. Austin: Bard Press, 2000.

Green, Meg. *Everything You Need to Know about Credit Cards and Fiscal Responsibility.* New York: Rosen Publishing Group Inc., 2001.

Guffey, Mary Ellen, Kathleen Rhodes, and Patricia Rogin. *Business Communication: Process and Product.* 4th Canadian ed. Toronto: Thomson-Nelson, 2005.

Page, John A.; O'Donnell, Jill; McWaters, Graham; *The Canadian Retirement Guide*, Toronto: Insomniac Press, 2004.

Scott, David L. *Guide to Managing Credit.* Old Saybrook: Globe Pequot Press, 1994.

Snyder Sarah. "Indebted students beware: employers checking credit." *The Lantern.* [www.thelantern.com] Ohio State University. 11 Apr 2003.

Bankrate.com [www.bankrate.com]; 15 Feb 2005.

CardWeb.com [www.cardweb.com]; 15 Feb 2005.

Credit Info Center [www.creditinfocenter.com]; 15 Feb 2005.

Credit.com [www.credit.com]; 15 Feb 2005.

Equifax Credit Bureau [www.equifax.com]; 15 Feb 2005.

Nation Credit Union Administration [www.ncua.gov]; 15 Feb 2005.

National Foundation for Credit Counseling [www.nfcc.org]; 15 Feb 2005.

TransUnion Credit Bureau [www.transunion.ca]; 15 Feb 2005.

www.alis.gov.ab.ca/studentsfinance/granttyp.asp; 15 Feb 2005.

www.alis.gov.ab.ca/studentsfinance/manrem.asp; 15 Feb 2005.

www.aved.gov.bc.ca/advanceded/sfa/scholarships.html; 15 Feb 2005.

www.aved.gov.bc.ca/studentservices/student/finish/debt_red/bc_nurse.htm; 15 Feb 2005.

www.canlearn.ca; 15 Feb 2005.

www.canlearn.ca/living/housing/place/clonCam.cfm?langcanlearn=en; 15 Feb 2005.

www.cra-arc.gc.ca/E/pub/tg/rc4092/rc4092-04e.pdf; 15 Feb 2005.

www.edu.gov.nf.ca/studentaidsystem/grants.htm#reduction; 15 Feb 2005.

www.familyresource.com/finance/21/697/; 15 Feb 2005.

www.gov.pe.ca/educ/index/php3?number=1000707&lang=E/re sources/index.asp; 15 Feb 2005.

www.macleans.ca/universities; 15 Feb 2005.

www.moneycentral.msn.com/articles/smartbuy/dollar-wise/7731.asp; 15 Feb 2005.

www.moneycentral.msn.com/content/savinganddebt/finddeal-sonline/p42610.asp; 15 Feb 2005.

www.moneycentral.msn.com/content/savinganddebt/save-money/p33731.asp; 15 Feb 2005.

www.moneycentral.msn.com/content/savinganddebt/save-money/p88487.asp; 15 Feb 2005.

www.moneycentral.msn.com/content/savinganddebt/save-money/p90000.asp; 15 Feb 2005.

www.moneycentral.msn.com/content/savinganddebt/save-money/p61288.asp; 15 Feb 2005.

www.moneycentral.msn.com/content/savinganddebt/save-money/p108552.asp; 15 Feb 2005.

www.moneycentral.msn.com/content/savinganddebt/travelfor-less/p106447.asp; 15 Feb 2005.

www.nwtsfa.gov.nt.ca/; 15 Feb 2005.

www.osap.gov.on.ca; 15 Feb 2005.

www.sayplanning.com/article/0,3868,2-10-0-9761,00.html; 15 Feb 2005.

www.sayplanning.com/saygoodcredit/budget_plans/living.htm; 15 Feb 2005.

www.scotiabank.com/cda/content/0,CID534_LIDen,00.html; 15 Feb 2005.

www.stretcher.com/stories/04/04feb23g.cfm; 15 Feb 2005.

www.studentaid.gnb.ca/pdf/guide-e.pdf; 15 Feb 2005.

www.studentloans.ednet.ns.ca/infor2004/info.shtml#funding; 15 Feb 2005.

www.theglobeandmail.com/generated/realtime/specialreport-card.html/home.asp; 15 Feb 2005.

www.thelantern.com; 15 Feb 2005.

http://www.canlearn.ca/living/housing/place/cloffcam.cfm?langcanlearn=en

Index